T0018202

THAT WAS
ZEN
THIS IS
TAO

THAT WAS ZEN THIS IS TAO

Living Your Way to Enlightenment

CHRIS PRENTISS

POWER PRESS

Los Angeles, California

Copyright © 2023 The Prentiss Trust of June 30, 1998. All rights reserved.
Printed in the United States of America. No part of this book may be used,
reproduced, translated, electronically stored, or transmitted in any manner
whatsoever without prior written permission from the publisher, except
by reviewers, who may quote brief passages in their reviews.

For information, contact:

Power Press®
6428 Meadows Court
Malibu, California 90265
E-mail: info@PowerPressPublishing.com

For foreign and translation rights, contact Yorwerth Associates
E-mail: nigel@publishingcoaches.com

ISBN: 978-0-943015-78-1

10 9 8 7 6 5 4 3 2 1

Library of Congress Control Number: 2023934723

Cover and interior design: Patricia Spadaro
"Consciousness Drained of Doubt" copyright © Dermot Obrien

Notes: What is contained herein is not part of the Taoist religion. Any
similarities or differences are coincidental. Any reference to *he* or *she* does
not exclude the opposite sex. Some of the names and details in the stories
in this book have been changed to protect the privacy of those involved.
The information in this book is not intended as a substitute for consulting
with a physician or other health-care provider. All matters pertaining to
your individual health should be supervised by a health-care professional.

The Chinese character 道 that is used opposite the first page of each chapter in this book is the character for Tao, meaning "the way" or "the path."

To my Irish friend
and poet Dermot Obrien,
who introduced me to the condition
"consciousness drained of doubt"

(Dermot's poem is at the back of this book)

Welcome to the Taoverse:
Everything, Everywhere, Eternally

A paraphrase from Plato's *Apology:*

"It is not living that matters
but living rightly."
—*Socrates (470-399 BCE)*

Contents

Your Path
to Enlightenment

"Enlightenment is knowing Who You Are in relation to All-That-Is."

1

....

Your Path
to Enlightenment

I've written this book to open you to the reality in which you truly exist and to provide you with information to brighten your days and nights so that whatever time is left to you on planet Earth will be more fruitful, happier, more peaceful, and less stressful. I'm also sharing what's here to help you create a deeper connection and communication with the spiritual essence of our created existence and to fill you with joy over the awareness of who you truly are, your journey through the millennia to arrive here, what your mission is now that you're here, and where you're going when your time to transition arrives, as it surely will.

I have just completed my eighty-sixth year on this lovely little planet. Throughout my adult life,

I've searched the world for the wisdom that has brought people lasting happiness and true success. I say "true" success because it is more than just success in the workplace, in the home, and in the material world. It's success as a human being and success in our relationship to the consciousness, the awareness that is Tao (pronounced "dow"). I have studied the world's most ancient writings that have been handed down through thousands of years and I have put into practice what I have learned about the natural laws that govern the lives of us all.

I've written several books based on that wisdom, including *Zen and the Art of Happiness,* which has been published around the world in many languages. In that book, I talk of the true meaning of Zen and how to apply its simple principles to achieve happiness.

The next step is *That Was Zen, This Is Tao.*

Because you are here seeking truth, spirituality, knowledge, and wisdom and because you are walking your path toward enlightenment, I salute you. *I bow low to you.* If I may be so bold as to say it, we are of the same family, the ones who work at being spiritual. I usually don't use the word *spiritual* because it is so powerfully associated with one or more of the forty-two hundred religions of the world, all of which were created by humans. The spiritual I'm referring to is the ethereal world, the heavenly world, the celestial world—the world beyond what is considered the physical universe. On that level, we are already friends, even if this is your first venture into that spiritual world.

We have probably had similar experiences, arrived at some conclusions about life on our planet, and are searching for more. We've individually evolved to this point in time where our destinies have brought us together.

Because of who you are, because this book has come into your possession, and because there are no coincidences in life, it *is* your next step. May this step bring you great joy, many blessings, and a huge enlightenment leap that will ease and illumine your passage on planet Earth.

A Bit of Information

This entire book is based on what I know to be true. That doesn't mean it *is* true. It just means that it is true to me. Because I speak from the certainty of my own experience, I rarely, if ever, use words such as *maybe, possibly, likely, could be,* or *hopefully.* Some of what you'll read came from what I call "*revela*tions," information that was revealed to me as I wrote. That revealed information came from the same source that reveals new ideas and new thoughts to you.

Every new thought you've ever had came from the same place as mine. Receiving information in the form of ideas, solutions, or creations is common to us all. All-That-Is provides new information to each of us to help light our way. To get the information, concentrate on what you need to know and be open to the thoughts that come, whether they come immediately or days or weeks later.

During our time together, I will occasionally call upon the wisdom that has been passed down to us from some of our greatest thinkers and visionaries from thousands of years ago. Sometimes I'll weave into our conversation stories that are mostly autobiographical as well as concepts about the laws of the universe. I'll also talk about some wondrous and useful facts from the world of science, but only as a way of showing you how miraculous and enchanting is Tao and the world in which we live.

When we talk about topics I believe are super-important to you, ones you may want to remember, I have set them off from the rest of the text. To get the most out of that information, perhaps read over those passages more than once. I invite you to print out those you find especially meaningful or relevant and place them where you spend time or save them in your device so that you can occasionally bring to mind a particular concept. Sometimes you may just need a boost in your day to remind you of *Who You Are* and *Where You Came From* and *From Whom*.

Here's one of those simple but immensely profound concepts that you can keep in mind throughout our explorations and that you'll see again in these pages:

> *To slow time down and add years to your life, practice enjoying the moment. It's where you spend your entire life.*

Our conversation will have some of the characteristics of an ocean wave traveling outward from the shore. It will start slowly, then build, grow larger, fuller, carrying us out to an uncharted ocean of ideas, facts, stories, concepts, and conclusions. I say carrying "us" because I am with you on this journey. *We are on this planet together.* So any advances, insights, and spiritual realizations you obtain benefit us all.

You may come across concepts and statements that are contrary to what you believe, contrary to any religion you follow, contrary to what you were taught by parents, teachers, and friends, contrary to what you learned from TV and the internet, contrary to information in books you've read, and even contrary to your common sense— *especially* contrary to your common sense. That is to be expected. If it weren't that way, there would be no point in our having this conversation.

For example, I make statements like this: *The entire created universe is alive, conscious, and aware.* There is no proof of that, and there are many highly respected people, learned and intelligent people, even some who are our most revered thinkers, who believe otherwise. But those people live in what, for them, is a dead, unresponsive universe.

Because some of the information may be new to you or contrast with your currently held beliefs, you may at first feel uncomfortable. Give yourself time to absorb and become familiar with the information. Some of your beliefs may have been, probably have been, with you since childhood. Smaller sessions are best. There are natural stopping points along the way.

At first, listening to some of the bold statements I make may cause you to scoff at what you heard, the ideas seeming not only stupid and implausible but impossible. You may want to trash the book, thinking it was a mistake to have obtained it. Before you do, ask yourself: *"Would I want what I've read to be true?"* And then, perhaps, allow yourself to discover through intuition, perception, imagination, openness, thought, and by reading ahead if it *could* be true or even if it *is* true. Imagine what *that* would be like.

If you are having trouble in some areas of your life or are feeling a bit of unhappiness, that could be because some of what you currently believe about life is not in keeping with the laws that govern our cosmos, one of which is that everything that occurs in your life will ultimately be of maximum benefit to you. Sometimes it just takes a small mental adjustment to set things right. Those are wonderful moments to experience. They cause us to smile a lot and, ultimately, to laugh a lot.

Welcome to the Conversation

I have written this as if I'm talking with you. Picture this . . . It's midmorning on a beautiful sun-filled day. As we walk together past the flower garden, the vegetable garden, the lake and into the forest, we come to a cathedral-like grove of trees to talk about existence and its wonders and about beliefs you may hold that may not be aligned with "what is." We will explore different aspects of life, spirituality, and the "Taoverse," a name I created to describe the space in which our so-called universe exists. More about the Taoverse a bit further along.

We are sitting comfortably on soft-cushioned, wooden easy chairs on a grassy lawn in the center of the grove. The branches of the broad-leafed trees arch above us. We hear the magical sound of a small waterfall as water runs over rocks that form the face of a small cliff before falling into a shallow pool. Birds are drinking and bathing, fluttering their wings as they splash water onto themselves, serenading us with their cooing and singing. The gentlest of breezes rustles the flowers that surround us. The sound of bees gathering honey provides the chorus.

Being here with you is a sublime experience (*sublime*: of such outstanding spiritual beauty or expression of intellectual and moral thought as to inspire great admiration or awe). It's a peaceful, happy time.

On the occasions when you take a break from our conversation, as you should, think about what I've said to see if the Taoverse you'll be hearing about is the real place in which you live. We will resume our talk in this space whenever you return, whether you have gone for a short break or a long one, even if it's for a second or third reading.

Whenever you join me here, carve out a bit of time when we won't be interrupted. During our talks, allow yourself to be open to the potential you'll hear about. Let down your guard. You can always go back to your old way of thinking, but for the few hours we will be together in this adventure allow yourself to experience something new—*something that has the potential to exalt you and reframe and refine your existence.*

I wish you the same joy, even exultation, in reading or listening to what's here that I experienced when writing it. Come along with me now and see if what follows resonates with you. Buckle up—it's the ride of a lifetime!

Why Tao?

Eight thousand years ago, when the air was completely clean and water sparkled fresh and pure from the earth, before writing or numbers existed, the great sages of ancient China conceived of the spiritual essence of All-That-Is. They referred to that spiritual essence as "The Creative." They believed the Creative was impossible to name or describe. They only knew it existed.

The sages spoke of "Tao" as the path that leads to living in harmony with the universe and which, if followed, would lead one to enlightenment.

*Enlightenment is knowing Who You Are
in relation to All-That-Is.*

As thousands of years crept by, the sages began

to talk about Tao not only as the path that leads to enlightenment but also as the unknowable, indescribable Creator of All-That-Is. As recorded in the first verse of the ancient Chinese classic called the Tao Te Ching: "The Tao that can be expressed in words is not the eternal Tao. The name that can be named is not the eternal name. The nameless is the origin of heaven and earth." Yet name the spiritual essence of All-That-Is I must if we are going to be able to talk about the consciousness that created All-That-Is and you and me—the spiritual essence I call Tao.

Many English-speaking people use the word *God* to describe what I call Tao. As I noted before, on our little planet there are roughly forty-two hundred religions that have been created, and we humans actually have thousands of names for God. God, however, is not a name; it's a generic description of a deity. Those who speak the English language are almost alone in calling their deity God. Nearly everyone else names their God, whether they use Zeus, Poseidon, Thor, Yahweh, YHWH, Father, Amen Ra, Jehovah, Elohim, Anu, Onkar, Sat Nam, Neptune, Thor, Allah, Dios, Jupiter, Jah, Ahura Mazda,

Aphrodite or Pele (goddesses), or any of thousands of other names.

When you're walking in the park with your friend and you see a statue of a great general who is easily recognized, you don't say to your friend, "Look, there's statue." You say, for instance, "Look, there's Napoleon." Seeing your friend's wife, you don't say, "Look, there's wife." You say, "Look, there's Patricia." You don't say to your friend when seeing one of your classmates, "Look, there's classmate." You say, "Look, there's Mary."

For me, the word *God* is too impersonal. I refer to my deity as Tao because I like the sound of it and because for thousands of years Tao has been the name for the path one follows to reach enlightenment. I learned the name Tao from my study of the writings of the Chinese sages and from the I Ching, the Chinese classic that is one of the world's oldest and most profound sources of wisdom. For the rest of our conversation, I will use Tao as the name for the Creator of All-That-Is. What All-That-Is *is* will be part of our conversation a bit later.

We have only had real writing for roughly five thousand years. Hieroglyphics, which uses pictures and symbols, dates back six thousand years—its creation credited to the Egyptian deity Thoth, also thought by some to be the architect of the pyramids. The concept of God existed much earlier. A bone carving believed to be that of a deity was found in Germany in 2008. It was created between 35,000 and 45,000 years ago. Homo sapiens, the first modern humans, evolved from our early great ape predecessors more than 300,000 years ago. We developed a capacity for language 50,000 to 100,000 years ago. The first modern humans began migrating out of Africa as much as 120,000 years ago.

Once upon a time, almost all of us lived in Africa. And we were all black. Did our early ancestors of a hundred thousand years ago sit in their caves, with thunder and lightning crashing around them, wondering if there was a "Great Being" in the sky who was causing it? Of course our ancient ancestors believed in one god or many gods. How could they not when their broken bones knitted, when they experienced glorious sunsets, their moon shrinking and expanding, their sun appearing and disappearing, the seasons revolving, their wounds healing, earthquakes shaking, babies being born, shooting stars, forest fires, lightning, droughts, thunder, snow, rain, and their own aliveness?

Earth's many cultures have had many gods: gods of fertility, harvests, water, animals, rain, and gods of all the natural phenomena.

It doesn't matter what names people of Earth use for their God. Everyone is talking about the same thing: the spiritual essence of the Taoverse.

If what you believe about God fits what I believe about Tao as the Creator of our Taoverse, then, yes, our God is the same, names only making them seem different.

You can use Tao as a name for God, use another name, or create your own name. I'm sure your deity will be wonderfully pleased with any name you choose, even if it's to continue calling your deity God. You don't need an intermediary to talk with Tao or whomever you perceive as your deity. Tao is fully present—always. Have a conversation with your God whenever you decide: *Dear God, I would like to talk with you more intimately and call you by name. I hope you will like it if I call you Tao or Dear One (or any name you choose).*

The Taoverse

Here's one of my bold statements: There is no such thing as "the universe." Here's an entirely new concept—*The Taoverse: Everything, Everywhere, Eternally.*

Taoverse, as I said, is a name I created to take the place of "universe." *Universe* is a word philosophers used thousands of years ago when writing about what they thought was "everything that existed." *Uni* means "one" and *versus* comes from the root word meaning "to turn," both derived from Latin. To me, its meaning is that "the One" turned into "our universe."

Scientists, including cosmologists, who study the origin and development of what they believe to be the universe, have traced cosmic history back 13.8 billion years to what they believed was the creation of "the universe": a small ball of incredibly hot, ultradense energy that exploded, creating "the universe"—an event that has come to be known as the Big Bang.

Albert Einstein (1879-1955) believed nothing existed prior to that event, no space and no time. He got out of that jam by stating that space and time were created as the matter and energy from the explosion sped outward in every direction. I believe this view is naïve, partly because scientists have not yet understood the true nature of Tao and how Tao works. *Naïve:* having or showing a lack of understanding, experience, judgment, or wisdom. Remember what *naïve* means as it will come up again. I love that word.

I believe that the part about the small ball exploding is true. However, that did not create "the universe." When the ball finally reached maximum density, it exploded in accord with Tao's law that when anything reaches its maximum potential, it turns toward its opposite—fullness to emptiness, hot to cold, high to low, maximum density to expansion. But the explosion didn't create a new universe; what happened was simply that a ball of energy exploded, propelling its contents into the limitless space of the Taoverse.

To imagine the Taoverse, first imagine the tiny part of it in which our supposed universe exists. Got that? Now take away the boundaries of that universe so it's just a miniscule part of the endless Taoverse in which trillions of balls of matter and energy may have been, and may still be, exploding, creating trillions of "universes."

The word *universe* suggests that the totality of created existence is a defined space. It's not. The ball we've been talking about exploded into already existing space—Tao's space. What resulted from that event is not a universe that is getting bigger and bigger, as scientists theorize, but just galaxies that are hurtling farther and farther into the endless space of the Taoverse, never to return— perhaps mingling with other galaxies from other Big Bangs or perhaps not, as the space into which they are hurtling is so vast that they may never meet up with galaxies from other Big Bangs. We'll return to these concepts again later.

Becoming an Ambassador of Tao

One of my goals for you, if you have not already achieved that goal, is for you to become a philosopher—one who questions, one who seeks after knowledge of the essential nature of our Taoverse, one who forms an opinion of "Who am I?" in relation to All-That-Is and who, as a philosopher, seeks to discover how it all fits together and then lives life accordingly as an ambassador of Tao and Tao's Taoverse.

Philosopher: a lover of wisdom, from the Greek *philos,* meaning "love," and *sophos,* meaning "wise"

Ambassador: a diplomat who is sent to represent a nation in a foreign country

After you have earned the title of "philosopher," you, as Tao's accredited diplomat, will live on planet Earth as Tao's "official representative in our Taoverse." It's not required that you accept the post, but the perks as well as the responsibilities are enormous.

Marcus Aurelius (121-180 AD), emperor of Rome and one of the great Stoic philosophers, said to the Taoverse: "Everything harmonizes with me, which is harmonious to you, O Universe. Nothing for me is too early or too late, if it is in due time for you." He also said: "What then is to provide good conduct for a man? One thing and one thing only: philosophy."

As true philosophers, we are following the path of Socrates, one of our original great philosophers, who was put on trial after being accused of blaspheming the gods and leading the youth of Athens astray. But what he was actually being brought to trial for was angering the powerful people of Athens by questioning them about their supposed area of expertise and exposing them as frauds in front of the young people of Athens, whose parents had sent their children to follow Socrates to learn from his wisdom and method of inquiry that to this day is known as the Socratic method of inquiry. On trial for his life, Socrates defiantly stated:

"The unexamined life is not worth living."

Take a moment to read that phrase again and contemplate that truth to get the full impact of what the master meant.

A master is one who sees beyond what is obvious. He sees the unseen, feels the unfelt, hears the unheard. He looks below the surface for what is hidden and so finds the great heartbeat of the Tao. He smiles, knowing it is his heartbeat, your heartbeat, our heartbeat.

It takes great courage to follow the spiritual path. Courage is necessary because you will need to throw overboard some of what you believe to be true and embark on an entirely new course. Not to worry—on this path, you will be provided with the necessary courage. You may not know that or believe it, but by the time we finish our conversation, you will *know* it and *live* it.

Tao's Intention for You

This is a book of concepts, ideas, my philosophy, insights from the distant past gathered from our great philosophers, and Taoversal laws—collectively what I call "knowings." These knowings make up the heart of the book. Knowings are "special knowledge of a cosmic nature that are revealed to an individual"—in this case, you. Each concept you absorb becomes a knowing.

By embracing the knowings, you will gradually become aware of a revealed Taoverse of which you are perhaps unaware—one that is intimately aware of you, is friendlier and more supportive than you may have imagined, and that governs its manifestations through unbreakable, eternal laws.

Tao unerringly guides you, pushes you, corrects you, rewards you, nourishes you, and cares for you.

Do you heal your cuts? Or do you watch as your cuts heal over a period of weeks without wondering about the miracle that is taking place? Do you heal your bruises or your burns? Overcome your illnesses? Beat your heart that pumps one and a half gallons of blood every minute, a million barrels of blood in the average lifetime? Do you filtrate (clean) your entire blood supply twenty-five times every single day? Do you digest your food? Create moisture on your eyes? Grow your hair, your eyelashes, your fingernails and toenails? Do you provide yourself with a totally new blood supply every two months and a new skeleton every ten years? Do you create two to three million red blood cells every second, ten billion white blood cells every day, and thirty-five thousand skin cells every minute? Do you process six hundred million bits of visual information in one minute?

Of course not. Those essentials and thousands of others are all done for you. Your body, the one provided to you, the one in which you live, the one that comes with a head-to-toe repair warranty serviced by your immune system, is on loan. And at some point, the loan will be called in. Will you have accomplished what you wanted?

We'll talk more about your physical ending later. Just know this:

You are not your body.

If you lose an arm or a leg, you are still you. If you replace your heart, your liver or a kidney, you are still you. You are not your brain, which is the storehouse for information and takes direction from your mind. So who are you?

You are consciousness, pure consciousness, eternally alive and living temporarily in the body that is provided to you as a home in which to live while you assimilate the lessons you have come here to learn, a body that provides you with the opportunity to demonstrate the degree to which you have learned those lessons. The greatest, most amazing, most beneficial gift to us from Tao *is* consciousness!

Tao also provides you with information and ideas, arranges meetings and opportunities, and pressures you with adversity when you have strayed from the evolutionary path that establishes your destiny on planet Earth.

The knowings will guide you on paths that at first may seem strange but are aligned with Tao's intention for you. *Yes, Tao has intention. And, yes, Tao has intention for you.*

When you are far enough along on your path of evolution, of enlightenment, you will learn how to create a destiny for yourself that will surprise and delight you all your remaining days on our planet. Yes, you can create a destiny for yourself—not the specifics of it, but the overall look and feel of it. Pretty special?

The knowings also offer solutions to problems, guidance during stressful moments, and power to obtain things. Knowings alleviate sadness, brighten darker moments, and provide insight into knowledge that sets you free—free from fear, free to achieve, free to become who you want to be, and free to bring your dreams into reality.

All fear is based on our expectation of a negative outcome.

As you progress along your path, instead of being worried or uncertain about your future, you will look forward to it with anticipation because you will live your life in accord with the laws of the Taoverse and in accord with Tao's intention for you, and therefore you will take actions that will create the future you desire.

Work diligently and courageously. Understand and activate what you find here and all will be well—changed for the better. The image you hold of yourself will be changed for the better. Your efforts will be changed for the better. Your results will be changed for the better. *You* will be changed for the better.

By the time we have completed what we have now begun, you will be more aware of the Taoverse in which you truly live, a Taoverse of which you are an inseparable part. You will live in the certainty that you are part of an aware, conscious Taoverse, that you are a golden child of an eternal Taoverse that is intimately aware of you and has your best interests at heart. For you and Tao are one.

Your Partnership
with Tao

"Your consciousness is the consciousness of Tao. You share consciousness. That means you are connected to, are part of, the greatest, most powerful source that exists."

2

....

Your Partnership
with Tao

Your consciousness is part of Tao's consciousness.
Once you become fully aware of that, the concept you hold of yourself will be altered. You will
think differently, *feel* differently, and *act* differently.
That is the most important concept of our conversation. As you become aware that your consciousness is part of Tao's consciousness, everything will
change for the better. You will manifest yourself
differently and respond to events differently. You
will *be* different.

Part of what we will accomplish in our talk
will be to rebuild your image of Who You *Think*
You Are. When you walk into a room full of
people, it is Who You *Think* You Are who walks
into the room and it is Who You *Think* You Are

who speaks and acts, not Who You *Truly* Are.

Your every word, your every act clearly expresses Who You Think You Are. If you think you're not a great talker, not particularly handsome or pretty or not a very interesting person, or if you believe that your accomplishments have fallen short of your expectations or that you have not lived an exemplary life, that will radiate from you as if you were holding up a sign with a description of yourself on it.

Change that. Always remember:

> *You have been chosen to be part of the*
> *Taoverse—to exist. And that makes you*
> *the equal of anyone.*

Your goal is to maintain that awareness. Being a part of the Taoverse is better than all the titles that exist—king, queen, princess, president, rock star, smartest person on earth, greatest movie star, grand exalted ruler—and better than all the worldly fame or accomplishments you could attain. Having been chosen to be part of the Taoverse makes you not only the equal of anyone but far more awakened than anyone who does not realize who she or he is.

To live life as an enlightened being takes continuous awareness of Who You Are.

The results of forming a new vision, a new realization of Who You Truly Are will have far-reaching effects in your life. You will take on and manifest a new identity. You will be more confident, more trusting, more aware, more capable. You'll think better of yourself, and you'll never feel alone . . . *because you're not.*

Know also that Tao does not like it if we disdain someone Tao has chosen to receive life. Yet keep in mind that you must use caution and exercise good judgment, as not all are as they should be.

It's now time for us to start the real work. Ready? Do this:

Take a deep breath and hold it to a slow count of five.

1 . . . . . 2 . . . . . 3 . . . . . 4 . . . . . 5 . . . . .

Exhale . . . . .

Let's begin.

If you didn't take a deep breath, that's your ego at work. Perhaps you should start from the beginning . . .

To you who took that breath and exhaled, *congratulations.* Let's continue our conversation.

You Are the Author of Every Next Moment

The aware, conscious Taoverse of which you are a part is governed by unbreakable, unchanging, eternal laws. Under the pen name Wu Wei, I have written several metaphysical books on the ancient Chinese book of wisdom known as the I Ching. Two of those books, *I Ching Wisdom Volume One* and *I Ching Wisdom Volume Two,* reveal Taoversal laws found in the I Ching. Many of the laws are stated simply along with a few lines of guidance so you can easily apply them to reach your goals and live your life in a way that will avoid the pitfalls that beset the path of the unaware. *I Ching Wisdom Volume One* explores this Taoversal law:

> *A situation only becomes favorable after one adapts to it.*

About that truth I wrote: "As long as you are angry or upset over an event, you will be unable to perceive its beneficial aspects and you may wear yourself out with unnecessary resistance. The event may have been (actually was and is) to your complete advantage from the first moment. Even happy turns of fortune sometimes come to us in a form that seems strange or unlucky. The event itself is just an event; the way you respond to the event determines its outcome in your life.

"Once an event has taken place, since you cannot alter the past, all that is left to you is your response. Why not respond as though the event occurred for your benefit? You will then immediately experience good feelings about the event, and by acting in accord with your feelings, you will help to bring about that end. Anyone who understands that concept will mount to the skies of success as though on the wings of a dragon."

No matter what circumstance you find yourself in, this is always true:

> *You are the author of every next moment—because you get to choose how you will respond in every next moment.*

Our path, of course, is also influenced by others whose actions affect us. While we're young, we're influenced by parents and teachers and, as we go through life, by friends and people in authority. Our lives are powerfully impacted by the wisdom (or lack of it) of those who influence us and by the wisdom and motivations of our leaders.

Sometimes leaders lead us into war or reduced living conditions and at other times into peace and prosperity. Power-hungry dictators are usually the worst influence and create the harshest reality in which to live. The soundest advice for a leader comes from Lao Tzu, the sixth-century BCE Chinese sage whose main work is the Tao Te Ching, which means literally "The Book of the Way (Tao) and Its Virtue."

Lao Tzu counsels those who would be wise leaders: "A sound leader's aim is to open people's hearts, fill their stomachs, calm their wills, brace their bones and so clarify their thoughts and fill their needs that no cunning meddler could touch them."[1] It's the cunning meddlers we must beware of. They are easily recognized by what they say and whether their message is one of peace or aggression, help or hindrance, benefit or detriment.

Regardless of early influences or the events taking place around you, you are a powerful being and you have the power to reinvent your world.

Tao's Favorite Tool

Another truth on the path to enlightenment:

Everything happens for a reason, and the reason is so you can be benefited. No exceptions.

Considering what's gone before in your life, you may have difficulty with the above statement. But if you want to obtain true happiness, it is essential that you adopt that understanding as one of the pillars of your philosophy.

I realize that because of the life you've lived, the experiences you've had, the injustices that came your way, the lies you've been told, the embarrassments you've had to endure, the disappointments you've had to bear, the seemingly unfortunate events you've experienced, and the losses you've suffered, you may not believe you live in a totally just, completely well-intentioned Taoverse that always holds your best interest uppermost in its consciousness. But that's because you may not be aware that Tao's favorite tool is adversity. By the time you've completed this journey, you will understand that truth.

There are two ways you move along your path toward enlightenment. If your actions are in accord with Tao's laws, you move along smoothly, almost effortlessly, achieving your goals and fulfilling your desires. If your actions are not in accord with Tao's laws, you are coerced by obstacles, pain, and unhappiness for the purpose of changing your motivation, your actions, and your way of life to bring you into a state of harmony with the laws of the Taoverse. In other words, although you may be enticed along your path by what you believe will bring you happiness, if what you want for yourself is not in your best interest or if some part of your awareness needs developing, you will be driven along your path by the application of Tao's laws in the form of adversity.

Tao provides you with adversity to give you strength—strength of body, strength of mind, strength of heart, strength of character—and terminates the situations and conditions it created in your life when they have served their purpose to benefit you. Tao will conclude your time on this planet when it is time for you to evolve to the next life phase. *And that is the miracle.*

It takes practice feeling "in tune with" and optimistic regarding the ever-unfolding events of your life. And because of all the seemingly negative, hurtful, traumatic conditioning you have undergone, it may be very difficult for you to change the way you think about events that seem strange, unlucky, or even heartbreaking. But if you take to heart the saying *"Everything happens for a reason, and the reason is so I can be benefited"* and practice it, as the days unfold you will find yourself living an ever-happier life, smiling more and, finally, laughing more.

We'll delve into that key concept in more detail in an upcoming chapter, but for now think about it this way: All flaws increase unto destruction. By that I mean that if the creation of Earth and its inhabitants was flawed, the Earth certainly would have destroyed itself over the last 4.6 billion years since Earth blew into existence. So that means that our Earth is perfect, as are you. But you may not know it yet.

I realize that I am direct and forceful at times, and perhaps by this time you might be feeling "pushed around" a bit. That's ego—*throw it overboard*. You're on a journey to reach a goal of unimaginable worth and promise, and you can't be burdened with cumbersome pride or ego.

Instead, concentrate on this: You *are* the Taoverse—a part of it. It's the greatest honor anyone can hold. *You were chosen.*

You Are Completely Cared For

You'll miss out on the best, most important part of life if you believe the only reason you're here on this lovely planet is because your mother gave birth to you. It will help if you remind yourself that your consciousness *is* the consciousness of Tao. *You share consciousness.* That means you are connected to, are part of, the greatest, most powerful source that exists.

Can you imagine that? It would be a very lonely world if there were no spirituality in it, if there were no Taoversal laws to govern every aspect of our lives and our world. I would be frightened to live in a world where Tao wasn't present. That would be a world where anything could happen at any moment: true chaos.

Yet true chaos does not exist. If it did, we would be in danger of imminent destruction, as the meaning of true chaos is that "anything" can happen at any moment. But fourteen thousand million years after the Big Bang, we're here. "Anything" (like destruction), didn't happen. *We happened*. And that was and is perfect.

Even if Earth disintegrates, along with us, we'll still be part of the Taoverse. We'll just transition. We are part of existence. Whether we are in this form or another, we are part of Tao—and if there's one bit of information you can be absolutely certain of, it's that *Tao takes care of itself. We are part of "itself."*

At this point, you may be wondering: "How can Tao be completely aware of me and every individual on Earth?" The Tao that created our Taoverse and can do anything *did* do everything, and still does.

Thinking about wars, bombings, the Black Death (the Plague) of the 1300s that killed as much as 60 percent of Europe's population, the HIV/AIDS pandemic of 2005 that took the lives of 2.8 million people, the flu pandemic of 1968 that killed one million people, the flu pandemic of 1918 that killed between 25 and 50 million people, the COVID-19 pandemic of 2020, and the fact that we number at the time of this writing more than seven billion seven hundred million individuals and how that fits into a universe of love and individual attention—thinking about all that will deter you from understanding this:

You are completely cared for individually. And you can only be on your path to enlightenment.

Whether you are lying in a gutter drunk or sitting atop Mount Fuji contemplating Tao, you are on your path to enlightenment. And there is no telling which of those two scenarios will bring you to enlightenment more rapidly. The speed at which you arrive at your enlightenment depends on you—your intentions and the knowings you acquire, whether you acquire them here or elsewhere. The Zen master Eihei Dogen (1200-1253 AD) wisely said: "If you cannot find the truth right where you are, where else do you expect to find it?"

Two-Way Communication with Tao

You and Tao are in a partnership. For most of us, only one of the partners is aware of that partnership.

The more aware you become of Tao and your partnership with it, the stronger the partnership becomes. Once Tao becomes aware that you are aware of it, which is instantaneously, life will be different, much different—better, much better. You will be aware of and in a two-way communication with All-That-Is.

The truth that you share consciousness with Tao means that your thoughts are not private. Tao is present, *fully* present, *fully* aware of you and your thoughts. It takes a bit of getting used to Tao being constantly aware of you, and it may seem strange at first that your thoughts are not private, that you are being led on a path. But after a while you'll be grateful for it.

We are all operating on the same wavelength of consciousness, Tao's consciousness. We are all joined together in it. Can you recall times that you were thinking of someone and the phone rang and it was that person calling you? Or times when you were going to say something and the person you were with said it, or vice versa? We've all had those experiences.

There is no lag time in the transmission of information between you and Tao. As the elder mentor of Jonathan Livingston Seagull (in Richard Bach's classic by the same name) tells his young apprentice: "Perfect speed, my son, is being there."

Consciousness is in your brain, your mind, your body. And because that is true, you are the transmission-and-receiving station for communication with Tao. Where do you think your new ideas come from, the ones you never had before?

Tao has always been, and still is, in communication with you. You are not now and never have been alone.

The difference now is you'll know it. The knowing of it takes practice. Once you come to realize that your awareness and knowledge are part of Tao's consciousness, your awareness of being tapped into Tao's consciousness will develop more rapidly, even as you are reading or hearing this. Maintaining your awareness will naturally result in an increased ability to maintain your awareness for longer and more frequent periods of time.

As you become more aware of the revealed Taoverse, the Taoverse will reveal more of itself to you. When you have understood more of the qualities of the Taoverse and how it works, you will have gained knowledge of what is true in the Taoverse and you can then perceive by intuition a proper course of action that will keep you aligned with Tao's intention.

Knowing Tao's intention for you, and conforming to it, will empower you to achieve goals that are beyond the reach of the uninitiated, the unaware, the unknowing and will make it possible for you to live in harmony with the great intention, the great awareness, the great consciousness that created you and the Taoverse.

Once you are at that point of being aware of and in communication with Tao, you will have a greater responsibility to live life according to higher principles. If you would be helped by Tao, make yourself worthy of help.

What It Means to Be on the Path to Enlightenment

You may want to take a moment to consider what it means to live according to the principles or laws of Tao and to be on the path to enlightenment.

Being "on the path" is to be aware of Tao,
to live according to Tao's laws and Tao's
intention for you, and to be a representative,
an ambassador of Tao in all you do.

Living your life according to principles that are not aligned with what is expected of an ambassador of Tao will result in living your life without the full benefits you could have if you were to embrace the principles of Tao.

What follows is one of the most important universal laws:

To be the recipient of what is highest and
best, you must live according to what is
highest and best.

Therefore, pettiness must go. Meanness must go. Taking advantage of others must go. Hating must go. Taking revenge must go. Manipulation must go. Giving-to-get must go. Using sarcasm or discourtesy to hurt people close to you and with strangers must go. Fabrication must go.

Unless you already speak the truth all the time, giving up lying will be very difficult. It takes courage, determination, and endurance. The rewards, however, are immense. Some people laugh at the idea of giving up lying. A reminder from Lao Tzu: You can always tell which is the true path: fools laugh at it.

Resentment, too, must go. You will never be able to experience complete happiness as long as you carry resentment for anyone or anything. Resentment diminishes happiness. They cannot occupy the same space at the same time.

Our mind cannot hold resentment and
happiness at the same time.

In a sense, it's actually an act of selfishness to give up resentment, because you are the one who benefits. If you would be happy, content, you must let go of regret and resentment. Any regret or resentment for what has been done to you or even for harmful things you have done to others dispels your happiness. What happened is done and cannot be undone, because you cannot change the past. What you can do is change the way you *think* about the past and what you believe to be true about the past.

You must learn from the past and be grateful for the lesson and move on, knowing the person or persons you harmed also had the opportunity to learn something for their growth and understanding. That is not to say that you will escape the results of your harmful deeds, but if you're sincerely sorry and have set yourself on this new path, your karma is softened and easily forgiven in the light of Tao's complete understanding.

If you have led a life that has not been aligned with what is right, good, just, and caring, a life not in keeping with the finer precepts of our Taoverse, you will find that those mean, thoughtless, harmful acts or activities, no matter how harmful or bad they may seem to you, are only trifles that can be easily overlooked in Tao's consciousness—*provided you have had a real change of heart.* You will find they are nothing more than slight digressions from the correct path, the path that has now led you to this conversation.

Look back over your life. *What were you like? What have you done? Where will you go now? What will you be like?*

Tao's
Cosmic Plan

*"You are a spiritual being endowed
with the essence of life, gifted with powers
beyond anything you may currently conceive.
Wake up! And that will be the miracle."*

3

....

Tao's
Cosmic Plan

The scientists of our modern era have made huge accomplishments in demonstrating with equations, formulas, and theories aspects of what they call the "universe." Many scientists, including Professor Albert Einstein in his general theory of relativity and in his famous equation $E = mc^2$ (where E stands for energy, m for mass, c for the speed of light, and ^{2} for the speed of light squared, or multiplied by itself) have greatly contributed to our understanding of the awe-inspiring cosmos in which we live. Congratulations to them all. What they have done and are still doing is demonstrating the laws of Tao.

Those formulas come in handy, for example, in predicting eclipses or developing new ways to harness energy. However, none of those equations or formulas touch on the most important aspect of our Taoverse: Taoversal *life,* Taoversal *consciousness,* Taoversal *awareness*—the part that provided us with life, the part that provided them with the information they discovered.

When the sum of all that our scientists have figured out has been explained, down to the tiniest, final detail, all they will have discovered will be a laundry list of the laws of the Taoverse explaining how everything works. Nothing more. Without recognizing or even mentioning Tao, who created and gave all of it life, there is nothing spiritual about it. It's like preparing a detailed architectural plan for the construction of a great house with a list of how all the gadgets work without mentioning the architect or builder.

The Source of All Information and Ideas

Einstein knew what it felt like to be the recipient of Taoversal information. In Walter Isaacson's brilliant biography *Einstein,* in which he captured the essential boy, student, man, lover, professor, father, and physicist, Isaacson writes: "One day during the 1930s, Einstein invited Saint-John Perse to Princeton to find out how the poet worked. 'How does the idea of a poem come?' Einstein asked. The poet spoke of the role played by intuition and imagination. 'It's the same for a man of science,' Einstein responded with delight. "It is a sudden illumination, almost a rapture."[1]

What Professor Einstein was describing is the feeling we get when a new idea appears in our mind. When that happens, we are experiencing being "tuned in," even if we don't know it, to the subtle promptings of the Taoverse when it releases a new idea, in some cases the release of information never before released to humans. It is the same rapture I experienced during my writing of this book each time I gratefully experienced a *reveal*ation.

All information comes from Tao's store of information, wisdom, and ideas. Those to whom the information is released benefit from it and sometimes pass on the benefit to others. Those who pass it on are celebrated as the creators of the information. However, they didn't "create" the information. They didn't "figure it out," even though it seems as if they did. They were chosen to be recipients of the information as they tuned in to the energy that surrounded their question. What an honor.

The same is true for me and what you are reading here. The same is true for you when you receive new ideas and new realizations. What we call a "revelation" is a correct term because the information or the idea is *revealed* to us. We downloaded it from Tao's bank of wisdom and information. When I read the above to my wife, Lyn, she said: "Some scientists make themselves the 'gods of information' and they make us the lowly peons, when actually we are all receiving cosmic information—all the time."

All new information comes from Tao.
All old information came from Tao.

Most people are unaware of that gift, that honor. They live in the world of "I did it." That's okay; it's just a lack of awareness. It would be wonderful when you get a new idea, one that you're grateful for, if you gave a nod to Tao, an acknowledgement. You will get more new ideas that way.

Einstein frequently mentioned that he didn't believe that "God played dice" with the universe.

What he meant is that we do not live in a world of chaotic randomness and utter uncertainty. I take from that statement that Einstein believed, as I do, that we live in a "created" universe. Einstein, explaining one of his beliefs to a young girl, stated: "Everyone who is seriously involved in the pursuit of science becomes convinced that a spirit is manifest in the laws of the universe—a spirit vastly superior to that of man."

In this chapter, I briefly describe what our greatest minds have accomplished in their quest to explain our universe and its origin. I have done my best to share up-to-date information as simply as possible, knowing, of course, that scientists are making new discoveries all the time. You do not have to fully understand the science that underlies these discoveries to appreciate the vast cosmic intricacy of the place Tao created as our home. But I felt it was important to share what you'll read here—first, to help you put your life and the opportunity Tao has given you into perspective and, second, to show you that the picture scientists have been able to put together so far is still not the whole picture. To understand more of the whole picture, we have to understand more about Tao.

The Big Bang

Scientists and cosmologists (astronomers who study of the origin and evolution of everything since the Big Bang) generally believe the question about how our universe got here has been answered with their theory of the Big Bang. Fred Hoyle (1915–2001) was an English astronomer who in 1949 first called it the "Big Bang." The name stuck because it is generally thought that the original center of our universe was a tiny ball that exploded, producing our universe.

Scientists say the approximate size of the ball was somewhere between a trillionth of an atom with hardly any mass at all to a ball the size of a city block, with scientists' favorite size being that of a soccer ball. I imagine that a teaspoon of that intensely concentrated core would weigh about as much as our Earth. Astronomers estimated the amount of time that has passed since the Big Bang by looking for the oldest stars and by measuring the rate of expansion of everything since the Big Bang and extrapolating back to that event—13.8 billion years ago.

Since everything in our universe is expanding

outward and away from everything else, astronomers and cosmologists believe that at the beginning, nearly 14 thousand million years ago, *all the matter and all the energy* in our two-trillion-galaxy universe with its trillions of suns and planets was contained in that tiny ball of "something" that exploded—that moments after the Big Bang a primordial soup developed out of which life eventually came into being (*primordial* means existing from the beginning).

Imagine an empty, round, black balloon with small white dots on it. The dots represent galaxies. As we inflate the balloon, the dots move away from each other and outward. That's what is happening in our Taoverse, which is why cosmologists and astronomers believe as they do. I chose black as the color of the balloon because Einstein's theory infers there was no light before the Big Bang; so as the matter spread outward, it created space and time and eventually light from the suns (stars).

Now we are going to talk about information that has been written about very little, and in some cases not at all, at least not to my tiny bit of knowledge. Fasten your mental seatbelt and prepare to expand the boundaries of whatever you have thought about the universe and how it came into being. What follows are some of those "bold statements" I warned you of.

Our Big Bang was not the first Big Bang.
Big Bangs have been banging away forever.

How It Happened— and Is Still Happening

Some scientists believe that there is more than one universe, which they refer to as "multiverses." However, few speculate how the first universe came to be—or how the other universes came to be . . . and are still coming to be. Before we talk about that, let's explore the concept of black holes. This will help you understand some of the conceptions and misconceptions about the "universe," time, space, and Tao that holds the key to it all.

A black hole is an area of space where the gravity at its core is so strong that nothing, no particles or even light, can escape it. It is like a giant vacuum cleaner except that it uses gravity instead of air to draw in particles (matter) from the space around it, whether they be stars, planets, debris, smaller black holes, even whole galaxies. It is thought that what scientists call a stellar black hole is created by the collapse of a massive star (all stars are suns) that grew old and cooled, contracting in on itself, creating an extremely dense mass at its core that created a field of gravity.

In the center of our Milky Way galaxy, 26 thousand light years away from Earth, is a massive black hole called Sagittarius A*. Astronomers estimate that it is four million times the mass of our Sun. We can't see it because, as I said, not even light can escape its gravity. Scientists can see where it is and about how large it is by observing the material swirling around it and the influence of the black hole's gravity on stars that are orbiting it.

Our astronomers have pictured a black hole as a funnel drawing in matter from one location, but that's because the only evidence they can see is from their vantage point, looking at it from one side. Black holes, in fact, are not "holes"; they appear to be holes because astronomers only see one side of them, not what is happening on the other sides. But the one side they can see is doing what all the others sides are doing—drawing in matter from every side of its core.

It's the exact opposite of what happened at the Big Bang. In the instance of the Big Bang, the core exploded in every direction, whereas in the case of a black hole, it is drawing in from every direction. Seeing what appears to be a huge black area drawing objects into it may make it look like a funnel, whirlpool, or vortex; but, again, that's because we only can see one side of it. Our astronomers and cosmologists can only imagine what a black hole must look like. All they see is a vast empty black space attracting matter.

The more a black hole draws in, the greater becomes the density and the greater becomes its gravitational reach. Newton's law says that if you have two objects and you double the mass of one of them, that doubles the gravity between those two objects. Applying this to a black hole, as the mass continues to increase, the core will eventually draw in sufficient matter to reach an infinitely dense state. At that point, the ball will explode, creating a Big Bang and the start of a "universe."

What I said in that last sentence is contrary to what some scientists believe about our black holes and our Big Bang. But remember, *according to Tao's law when anything reaches its maximum potential, it turns toward its opposite: full turns to empty, hot to cold, war to peace, ultimate density to expansion—explosion.* Without taking Tao into consideration, it is not possible to re-create the beginning of our so-called universe and talk about how it came into existence, certainly not with equations and numbers.

I believe that the ball that exploded creating the original Big Bang, the first of what may have become trillions of Big Bangs, was willed into existence by Tao. The balls that exploded creating the successive so-called universes, including ours, were the result of black holes forming and their cores becoming ever-denser until reaching maximum density and exploding in accord with Tao's law. You might want to read this paragraph again.

Black holes create Big Bangs and, like farmers cultivating fields and raising livestock, Tao cultivates and populates the Taoverse. *That's right: Tao is a farmer.*

In 2019, in an unprecedented collaborative effort, scientists unveiled the first-ever image of a black hole, which was created by linking up a network of telescopes from around the planet and focusing in on a black hole located 55 million light-years away from Earth (a light-year is the distance light travels in one year—5.88 trillion miles, or 9.46 trillion kilometers). See the links listed in the following endnote to take a look at the image and learn more about it.[2]

Remember, though, they were still basically looking at only one side of it. To get a more accurate idea of a black hole in operation, imagine a plain silver ball about as big as a soccer ball floating in the air surrounded by a huge cloud of BBs such as you would put in a BB gun. Now make the ball magnetic and watch as it attracts the BBs closest to itself. As the BBs are drawn to the ball from every direction, they coat the ball with themselves, creating a larger, denser core with a greater gravitational reach.

The more BBs the ball draws in, the stronger becomes its magnetization, drawing in BBs from farther and farther away. As the BBs are drawn in, they pack themselves tighter and tighter, squeezing out all the space caused by their roundness until the ball reaches an infinite number of BBs, crushing them into an infinite density, at which time it explodes, blasting its life-containing matter in every direction. That's what it's like.

A Matter of Perspective, Perception, and Awareness

We humans manage endless time using seconds, minutes, hours, days, years, decades, centuries, millennia, and eons, all of which we created so we could make plans and record events. Nothing exists without time, within which everything exists.

Yet our perception of time is flawed.
Time doesn't move, and neither do
we move through time.

I know it's hard to conceive, perhaps impossible to conceive, but time has always been. We are talking about trillions of trillions of trillions of years and beyond, without a beginning. No beginning and therefore no end. And *that* is the miracle. And always, Tao has been planting and populating Big Bangs.

Time just *is*. What I call the Taoverse *is*: Everything, Everywhere, Eternally. We'll explore the idea of time more deeply in the next chapter.

This is a good time to reflect on my statement that each concept you absorb becomes a knowing.

Because two objects cannot occupy the same

space at the same time, we conceived of the concept of *before* and *after*, making "time" necessary. We perceive things growing, things dying, ourselves aging, mothers of every species birthing, seasons revolving, days and nights alternating, vegetation growing, the sun and moon seeming to rise and seeming to set when it's really just what is being revealed to our sight as the earth rotates. It's not really a sunrise or a moonrise. It's a sun reveal and a moon reveal. It's all a matter of perception and perspective—actually, a matter of awareness.

Here's another example. Our Sun is huge in relationship to the size of Earth. More than one million Earths can fit inside our Sun. Our Sun makes up more than 99.8 percent of the mass of our solar system. Our planets and some debris make up the rest of our solar system and account for just about one quarter of one percent of our solar system's mass. In your mind's eye, picture an Earth-sized flaming ball. Now picture eight butterflies one hundred miles away from the flaming ball that are flying in a vast circle, orbiting the ball. It takes them one year to orbit the ball. That scale is not accurate, but it will give you an idea of how small the planets are in relationship to our Sun.

Considering the composition of our solar system, the chances that we even exist are minute. Being roughly 93 million miles away from Earth, our Sun is *exactly* the right distance to create life on Earth as we know it—frozen in the north and south with wonderful glaciers and animals adapted to the cold and, at the equator, steaming jungles, rain forests, and an abundance of vegetation and animals adapted to the heat.

Space is also a concept we derived from our perception. It seems to us that all objects and phenomena—galaxies, planets, stars, us—"exist" in "space." Like time, space has always existed. Space and time are bound together. Actually they are more than bound together. Space and time are both manifestations of Tao's consciousness.

To be totally clear, everything is an aspect of Tao's consciousness.

That includes space and time and even what scientists call "dark matter" and "dark energy." You may not know that only about 5 percent of what we call our universe is made up of ordinary matter and energy. About 68 percent is made up of what scientists call dark energy (named "dark" because it's unknown), and 27 percent is made up of dark matter (named "dark" in this case because it doesn't interact with light and is therefore undetectable). Whatever dark matter and dark energy are (and no one knows what they are or what their purpose is), they, too, are a manifestation of Tao. They actually *are* Tao. Not all of Tao, but *all Tao*.

The first of Newton's laws is that in a vacuum, an object at rest stays at rest and an object in motion stays in motion, maintaining the same speed in the same direction unless acted upon by an external force. Let's apply that to the Taoverse.

According to the laws that are operative in our Taoverse, when an explosion occurs, matter and energy rush outward in every direction, first going faster and faster until they reach maximum velocity and then gradually slowing down due to the friction of air and the force of gravity until the energy is fully dissipated and the motion stops. Yet according to our astronomers, the speed of our farthest galaxies is increasing. It would be a violation of Newton's laws if the speeding up of the galaxies was not being caused by something.

There is speculation that dark energy is responsible for the acceleration. If something is causing the galaxies to accelerate, I believe it is equally possible that in space there is something *drawing* the galaxies ever faster the nearer they get to it rather than something pushing them ever faster. Remember that the explosion of the Big Bang blasted matter away in every direction by propulsion. So whatever is now accelerating the speed of our outer galaxies is doing so from every direction.

Here's a bit of fantasy: It could also be that our galaxies are speeding up with the sheer exuberance of flying into space. Or maybe they're on the way to a rendezvous and, as they get closer, they speed up due to the anticipation of getting there. There is one thing you can be absolutely certain of: *Whether they are being drawn or pushed, Tao is responsible for it through natural law!*

Equations Can't Provide the Answer to Everything

The scientific theory of how it all began with the Big Bang doesn't answer the questions "Who or what created the ball that exploded, creating the so-called universe?" and "What was there before the ball was there?" Most important, it does not answer questions about life or consciousness, although scientists' theories attempt to uncover some answers about life.

You will see once more here that what our scientists are describing are the physical aspects of how they speculate life came into existence, leaving out the spiritual aspect. Again, by "spiritual," I don't mean "religious." When I use the word *spiritual,* I'm talking about the world of Tao—the celestial world, the heavenly world, the world of infinite space, the world of infinite time—not the world of our forty-two hundred religions.

Earlier I said that scientists have speculated that life did not exist before the Big Bang or at the moment of the Big Bang. That is a narrow, unenlightened view of existence based on theories derived from scientific experiments that led them to their assumption that life did not exist before the creation of our universe and neither did space, time, or anything else—zero. So according to these scientists, "nothing" gave birth to creation. Even children could figure out that that can't be right, especially children.

The problem with scientific speculations is that the correct answers to our questions will always elude us as long as we continue using equations to attempt to explain what can only be perceived by the mind using its faculty to perceive input from Tao.

Professor Stephen Hawking (1942-2018) was a theoretical physicist, cosmologist, author, and director of research at the Centre for Theoretical Cosmology at the University of Cambridge in England. He was one of those looking for the answer to the question "How did it all become?" I sent him an email where I said: "What you are looking for is not in the sandbox in which you are playing." I didn't get an answer.

Many things cannot be expressed with numbers and equations. *What is the equation for a thought? What is the equation for when you die? What is heaven like? Do dreams exist before we get them? What is the equation for an idea? What equation represents a waterfall? What is the equation for love?* Those and thousands of questions like them cannot be answered with numbers or equations. Neither is there an equation for how our Taoverse came to be.

In 2011 Stephen Hawking said in an interview:

"I regard the brain as a computer which will stop working when its components fail. There is no heaven or afterlife for broken-down computers; that is a fairy story for people afraid of the dark." He was talking about the afterlife and whether there is a part of us that lives on.

Considering Hawking's situation, with early-onset motor neuron disease (ALS) that over decades paralyzed his body so that he was scrunched down in his wheelchair, talking with a voice-assisted device, needing assistance for every aspect of his life, I can understand why he did not want to be a believer in a life after death. Since this lifetime had treated him so harshly, I believe he didn't want there to be an afterlife or a next life where the same thing could happen.

Now that Stephen has passed on from the physical realm, he is experiencing the answer he was seeking. I wrote "What you are looking for is not in the sandbox in which you are playing" to Stephen because one cannot find or express the truth of the afterlife or how we existed before this life with an equation. It may be that the closest we can come to expressing it numerically or mathematically is 1 since *all is one,* perhaps divided or multiplied by infinity or eternity.

Everything Is Alive

To further understand how life came to be, we need to start with two definitions, of *organic* and *inorganic.* Regarding vegetables, which we are not concerned with here, *organic* means they are produced without the use of synthetic pesticides, sewage sludge, synthetic fertilizers, genetically modified organisms, bioengineering, or ionizing radiation and are grown in soil that has never been treated with chemical fertilizers and pesticides or at least for a certain number of years. Inorganic foods use some or all of the above to produce the finished food products. In chemistry, which we *are* concerned with here, *organic* means derived from living matter. *Inorganic* means not derived from living matter.

Our scientists have created many theories, many possibilities about the advent of life, none of which have they been able to prove. Their short answer regarding life is that life was not present at the moment of the Big Bang but came about billions of years later when a "soup" of inorganic (nonliving) matter came into contact with a (nonliving) carbon atom and *POOF!* became alive.

Simply stated, in chemistry the difference between organic (living) compounds and inorganic (nonliving) compounds is the addition of a nonliving carbon atom. Since I believe that life cannot evolve from nonliving, inorganic matter— no matter what nonliving, inorganic matter is added to it—and scientists have not proven their theory that life was created by the addition of a nonliving carbon atom to nonliving inorganic compounds, I give no credibility to their theory. Life cannot spring from nonlife.

All they have discovered is that nonliving matter does not contain a carbon atom and living matter does. That does not prove that the addition of a carbon atom to nonliving matter creates life, only that living matter contains a carbon atom. There must be intervention by *a living entity capable of endowing nonliving matter with life*. Actually, my belief is even broader than that. I believe nonlife does not exist.

Everything that was created came from, comes from, was part of, and is Tao and was alive to begin with. That is the only possibility in Tao's creation.

What our scientists and biologists were and still are attempting to do is to explain how non-life became alive, how the atoms we are made up of "woke up." *But everything is alive and always has been.* Just because you cannot see aliveness in a rock does not mean the rock doesn't have it. The rock is made of atoms. Inside each atom is a furious realm of activity with its neutrons and protons forming a nucleus around which electrons orbit at speeds that can travel around the earth in a little over 18 seconds. And just because cosmologists and other scientists have not been able to discern life in their imagined moment when the ball exploded in the Big Bang does not mean it was not present. It only means they have not been able to detect it.

The Mystery of Space

Cosmologists refer to the Big Bang as a "singu-larity." Wikipedia describes singularity as "infinite density before quantum fluctuations caused the

Big Bang and subsequent inflation that created the Universe."[3] Inflation in that context means the rapid expansion of space immediately after the Big Bang.

To me, the concept of space expanding seems ridiculous. Space is already fully expanded without boundaries. To imagine otherwise is the same kind of thinking as the concept humans used to have that the world was flat and that if we reached the edge of the world, we would fall off.

As I said, scientists, including Einstein, start with the theory that space did not exist before the ball exploded, that the ball existed in *nothing,* that it was the *only* thing that existed. A ball without space and without time. That must be the greatest magic trick of all existence. It's like pulling a rabbit out of nothing—no hat. But if there was no hat, there would be no rabbit because the rabbit existed in the hat. Same thing for the ball that exploded: No space, no ball. No time, no anything.

What is our so-called universe expanding into if it is not already space? We'll solve that in a moment. It gets increasingly interesting.

If what Professor Einstein claimed is true— that space and time were created when the ball exploded and sped outward—that means that space and time are still being created as our galaxies continue to stream outward in every direction. Do you think that our outermost galaxies are still creating space and time as they fly outward from the Big Bang? That would mean that every one of our furthest galaxies is still doing that individually—creating their own "space pockets." Or did they stop doing that? If they did stop doing that, where did the space they are moving into come from?

In some circles, there exists controversy over whether William Shakespeare was the author of the works that are credited to him. This answer, attributed by some to Mark Twain, satisfies me: "The works of William Shakespeare were written by William Shakespeare or someone else of the same name." Borrowing from Mark we could say: "What our universe is expanding into is space or something else of the same name."

Einstein realized that space is not "nothing." He was certainly right about that, but he didn't know what space is. Let's return for a moment to something we explored earlier that applies here.

As you now know, we are connected to, are part of, the consciousness of Tao. That is true even from the first instant, even in the womb. Our biologists and doctors tell us that when we are in the womb, we develop consciousness; but biologists and doctors do not know and therefore do not tell us the most important part about consciousness. What we actually develop is the ability to *perceive* consciousness, Tao's consciousness, even in the womb—especially in the womb—and to partake of Tao's wisdom, knowledge, guidance, and all else Tao makes available.

Consciousness pervades every particle of our Taoverse. Consciousness is in our stars, our moons, our stardust. It is in every cell of our developing bodies. The sperm and the egg are conscious. And in case you're wondering, you are composed of approximately 97 percent stardust.

Tao's consciousness is in every form that exists and doesn't exist. It exists as time; it exists as no-time. It also exists as ether.

It is ether that light as a particle (a photon) passes through, and it is ether that permits the flow of photons as a wave. Ether is also light itself. It is ether through which gravity exerts its influence, and ether is also gravity itself. And it is ether that we call space. Ether is the space within which everything exists, including the space inside a vacuum.

Consciousness and Ether

More than two thousand years ago, the Greek philosophers began talking about aether (now usually spelled "ether"). They thought it was the rarefied air in heaven that the gods breathed as opposed to the ordinary air we mortals breathe. Aristotle (384-322 BCE) brought this concept of "heavenly air" into the world of physics. His philosophy included aether as the fifth element, after earth, air, fire, and water. As part of his theory of the cosmos, Plato (approx. 428-348 BCE) wrote that there are different kinds of air and "the brightest part is called the aether."

The use of ether to describe that notion was popular during the seventeenth and eighteenth centuries, including a theory proposed by Johann II Bernoulli (1710-1790), who was recognized in 1736 with the Prize of the French Academy. In his theory, *all space* is permeated by ether containing excessively small whirlpools.

As we can read in Wikipedia, "In physics,

aether theories (also known as ether theories) propose the existence of a medium, a space-filling substance or field, thought to be necessary as a transmission medium for the propagation of electromagnetic or gravitational forces."[4]

Isaac Newton (1643–1727), developer of the laws of motion and gravitation, said that ether is "the perfect elixir...fragrant and healthy." Newton imagined it was what filled up space, which is true but stops short of the complete answer. Nikola Tesla (1856–1943) also talked about ether. In 1937, Tesla said that "all attempts to explain the workings of the universe without recognizing the existence of the ether and the indispensable function it plays" were and would always be "futile." I also believe that is true but that ether is more than he suspected it to be.

In 1887, an experiment to detect the existence of ether was performed by two famous physicists, Michelson and Morley. The experiment, named the Michelson-Morley experiment in honor of its authors, shocked the scientific community by yielding results that implied the nonexistence of ether. So, although our greatest thinkers who were searching for that universal element that filled all space, welded everything together, and made it possible for light and gravity to move through space had frequently turned to ether as the answer, they all finally abandoned that solution as incorrect and none came up with a definitive answer.

The reason no one came up with the answer is the same reason that I wrote in my communication to Stephen Hawking: *"What you are looking for is not in the sandbox in which you are playing."*

Scientists are looking for a substance to fill all of space, a substance that will permit light to travel as a wave, and a substance that permits gravity to operate between masses. Ether does all that and much more but is undetectable without taking into consideration Tao's consciousness, which *is* the answer to all the questions. In other words, scientists are using the tools of physics, which cannot detect the answer, instead of using metaphysics, which can.

Meta means "after," "beyond," or "transcending," and *physics* is the natural or the physical world. Metaphysics, then, is everything that transcends the physical world. Using only the tools of the physical world to find answers to our questions about life is like trying to unlock a door using a banana instead of a key, or like using an equation to understand love or sympathy or a thought about Tao.

As philosophers before us have suggested, ether also records the history of our Taoverse without which we would not have a past to remember. It is ether that permits the recording of all events within itself and makes possible the passage and transmission of "things" through it. Ether holds the constantly shifting destiny of our Taoverse and everything in it, including us. It is the storehouse that contains all of it—everything. It is the substance through which our thoughts are transmitted to others, and it is the thoughts themselves. Ether holds the two trillion galaxies resulting from our Big Bang and trillions of trillions more from other Big Bangs in the Taoverse.

What is it, then, that can do all those things? We can call it ether or aether to satisfy those who are searching for it, but it is *Tao's consciousness.* All the things in the world—houses, buildings, bridges, pyramids, knives, cars, beds, clothing, planes, pajamas, our thoughts, the inspirations that come to us—it's all Tao.

Tao not only contains everything,
Tao is everything.

But Tao can only be perceived by intuition. By being open to what is now being made available to you and because you have come so far and because it is the moment in time for it, you can perceive Tao, if only dimly. When you do, it's among the top experiences of all experiences.

There are moments in our lives we cherish, the odd moments when our awareness sharpens and we experience bliss. Perceiving you are Tao, a part of it, is one of those moments.

Particles That Heal and Energize

Another miracle to contemplate as you ponder the wonder of Tao and the Taoverse is the neutrino. Neutrinos are subatomic particles emitted from the core of our Sun. They are flowing through us constantly. And they are *really* small. How small is a neutrino? If a neutrino were to enter one end of a solid bar of lead a million miles long, it is unlikely it would touch anything before it exited the other end. That's mainly due to the fact that a neutrino has hardly any mass and no electrical charge.

Neutrinos come from the core of our Sun and from the core of every star in our galaxy close enough for its neutrinos to have reached us. Since there's hardly anything in space to stop neutrinos and since we are receiving them from not only our Sun but from other stars in our galaxy, the amount of neutrinos constantly passing through us is impossible to know. Scientists estimate that one hundred trillion neutrinos (100,000,000,000,000) pass through us every second, no matter where we are, day or night. To conceptualize a trillion: One trillion seconds is almost 31,689 years. One hundred trillion seconds is nearly 3,168,874 years.

We are as awash in neutrinos as we are in air, except the neutrinos are flowing through us and at nearly the speed of light. At any given second, asleep or awake, wherever we are, we are solidly packed with neutrinos constantly flowing through us.

Because no biologist or scientist of any discipline can detect any effect at all from the trillions of neutrinos passing through us every second, they state that the neutrinos have no effect on us.

How can it be that one hundred trillion neutrinos pass through us every second with *no effect*? More naïvety.

I believe that neutrinos impart maintenance of life and healing to us and that they supply energy to us, to our planet, and to everything else in our Taoverse. I believe those infinitesimally small particles energize our oceans and all water and bring vitality to the land and everything else they pass through or occasionally touch, possibly even bringing us information. I believe they vitalize the earth and give vitality to us as well as to vegetation.

Before I drink a glass of water, I hold it high above my head and ask Tao to potentize it. I imagine the water sparkling, vibrant with healing energy. I visualize trillions of neutrinos speeding through it, energizing it, endowing it with potency and love—love because it is a gift of Tao. And then I slowly drink it—sipping it, relishing the sweet taste of it, relishing the coolness of it, the feeling it creates as I swallow it, one sip at a time. I actually visualize the vital essence in the water being sent to various parts of my body, energizing and healing those parts. That potentized water, sparkling with healing, is *alive*.

Try it now. Take a glass of water, hold it up high just for a few seconds and ask Tao to potentize it. Visualize trillions of neutrinos gliding through it, causing the water to sparkle and turn into healing energy from Tao. Drink the water . . . slowly, as I described above. You'll be amazed at the feelings that brings. If parts of you need maintenance or healing, as you swallow the water one mouthful at a time visualize the water, now sparkling, shimmering with healing energy and vitality, going to those areas, healing them, energizing them. Visualize those areas healing and healed.

You can do the same thing with the air you breathe. *Healing balm is in the very air you breathe.* Mentally focus your attention on the part of you that needs healing. Now slowly take a deep breath, slowly filling your lungs to capacity while you send the oxygen to the part of you that needs healing. Now slowly breathe out, visualizing the ailing part being healed.

One minute is enough. Actually, one breath can be enough. Do that several times a day. Touch also helps. Touch the ailing part and just hold it, seeing it being healed in your mind's eye, asking Tao to help. You are Tao's creation. You are owed the help.

> *You are a spiritual being endowed with the*
> *essence of life, gifted with powers beyond*
> *anything you may currently conceive.*
> *Wake up! And that will be the miracle.*

As I'll emphasize again in these pages, there is nothing in this creation more this creation than you. You were here or there or somewhere before this creation came into being. You always were. You will always be.

Light and Darkness

Light is one of the greatest attributes of our gloriously alive, bright universe. The speed of light in a vacuum is 186,282 miles (299,792 kilometers) per second. That's roughly 670,616,629 miles (1,079,252,848 kilometers) per hour.

To get an idea of the speed of light, clap your hands together with intervals of roughly one second between claps. Do that now: *1, 2, 3, 4, 5.* In each interval, light travels around our Earth almost seven and half times. How far is it around Earth? Just about 24,901 miles (40,075 kilometers). In one 24-hour day, light travels more than 16 billion (16,000,000,000) miles (25,749,504,000 kilometers). Telescopes in outer space have collected light from galaxies that took 13 billion light-years to reach us.

To put the size, the immensity, of our Milky Way galaxy into a bit of perspective: If every lifetime you lived a hundred years, and every day of every lifetime you traveled 16 billion miles, to cross our Milky Way galaxy would take you a thousand lifetimes. And that is just our galaxy. At latest count, there are roughly two trillion galaxies in our part of the Taoverse, many much larger than ours.

Yes, our galaxy is *really* big and, according to our astronomers, getting bigger every instant as galaxies travel outward, away from their starting point of the Big Bang.

All this might give us pause to consider that in relation to the rest of the Taoverse, our planet is relatively about the size of an atom on Earth. And we, we are too insignificant to be relative to anything. Yet here we are, talking about philosophy, existence, consciousness, spirituality, and things we consider of great importance. How unusual and amazing is that?

Think of this: In order for there to be light, there must first exist non-light or total darkness. Nowhere in the Taoverse would there be light. No stars. Zero light. The blackest of the black. Therefore *light exists in total darkness.* The stars (suns) light up the Taoverse.

Can you imagine total darkness? No light from electricity, fires, candles, lanterns, suns? But for Tao, that's what we would live in—total darkness. Actually, without Tao, we wouldn't live at all. And because we obtain warmth from the light, without the warmth from our suns, it would be cold, really cold.

Our atmosphere extends outward from our planet up to 6,200 miles (10,000 kilometers). Outside of our atmosphere, the temperature is minus 454.75 degrees Fahrenheit (minus 270.42 degrees Celsius). And here I am, living comfortably on my little spot on Earth with the average temperature roughly 70 degrees Fahrenheit (21 degrees Celsius) entirely surrounded by a temperature of minus 454.75 degrees Fahrenheit on a planet that is spinning at the equator at roughly

1,000 miles per hour (1,600.3 kilometers) and circling our Sun at about 67,000 miles per hour (107,000 kilometers), carrying its atmosphere and moon with it! And planet Earth, along with the rest of our Milky Way galaxy, is hurtling approximately 390 miles per second (627 kilometers per second), or some 1.4 million miles per hour (more than 2 million kilometers per hour), away from its original starting point of the Big Bang.

If our atmosphere were to dissipate, we would all instantly freeze. If you jumped off a rock ten feet high, when you hit the ground you would smash into a million pieces. *Not to worry; you are pure consciousness. You would just transition.*

While we're on the subject of light, you may not realize that you've never actually "seen" a tree, your parents, your friends, the sky, water, clouds, a table, the earth, a dog, a book, a house, the moon, a flower, a human being, not even yourself. All you have ever seen are light rays reflected from those objects into your eyes, not the objects themselves.

You've never seen anything in its original state because the original object is the essence of Tao. It is Tao. And Tao does not permit us to see it, only its manifestations.

The Power of Your
Thoughts and Feelings

One further aspect of light, sight, and us is that when we look at something, just by observing it we subtly change it. We cause changes by what we're thinking when we look at things, particularly people. By looking into the heart of a flower with admiration, with appreciation for its beauty, its fragrance, its exquisite colors, we stimulate the flower.

In an experiment in 1966, one of many to follow, Cleve Backster, a polygraph expert, hooked up his polygraph instrument's galvanic-skin-response detector to the end of a leaf. As he thought about burning the leaf to gauge the plant's response—without even taking any physical action at all—the plant registered a wildly negative reaction, demonstrating to him that plants can perceive and respond to human thoughts and emotions.

When you look at others with contempt, envy, hatred, maliciousness, lust, or with an intention to hurt them, you can bring about change in them. Your thoughts and feelings can diminish them on the subtlest of levels. The same goes for love. Looking at someone with genuine love causes them to glow, to feel secure. It causes them to radiate warmth, congeniality, happiness, and comfort, and it heals them, cleanses them, and improves them. It also endears them to us and we, in turn, are cleansed and healed. When we are proud of someone, they bask in the glow of our appreciation, as do we when we are appreciated.

It's a fortunate child who grows up with mom or dad's reassurance: "You're wonderful, and I love you." When seeming misfortune strikes, that comforting message is there, encouraging, healing, and protecting: *"You're wonderful, and I love you."*

Not only do our thoughts affect others; our thoughts also affect us—particularly us. Émile Coué (1857-1926), a French psychologist, advised his ailing patients to repeat the mantra "Every day, in every way, I'm getting better and better." He suggested it be repeated as many as twenty times a day. He reported great success among his patients who rigorously followed his suggestions and thereby activated their subconscious healing mechanism.

René Descartes (1596-1650), the French philosopher, mathematician, and scientist known as the father of modern philosophy, stated: "I think, therefore I am." Carrying Descartes' thought to the next logical conclusion, you can say: "I'm alive, therefore Tao is alive. I'm conscious, therefore Tao is conscious. I'm aware, therefore Tao is aware."

Your Taoverse is alive, conscious, and aware.
All of it—every atom, every neutrino.

There is no such thing as death, only transition, forms flowing . . . seamlessly. One form becoming another, endlessly. An eternal flowing, flowering *of which you are a part.*

The Greatest Honor

Our consciousness is Tao's consciousness. We partake of its life, knowledge, and information. Since everything came from, comes from, *is* Tao, everything in our Taoverse is alive.

Having heard that, you may wonder: Are there other planets like Earth? It's estimated that there are at least one hundred billion planets just in our Milky Way galaxy. Are many of them millions or billions of years older than our little planet Earth? Of course. Do some of them support life?

Of course. Do their inhabitants have intelligence? Of course. Greater than ours? Some do, some don't.

Have some of them harnessed their sun's energy? Of course. Have they developed atomic energy? Atomic weaponry? Of course. Are some of them more highly advanced than we are? Have they developed space travel? Of course. Are they peaceful toward aliens? Some will be, others will not be.

You should know that we are not alone. But should we be concerned? No, not at all. Besides, we're so infinitesimal in such an immense space, it's extremely unlikely we will be noticed. And we have enough to be concerned about right here, where in thousands of years we have not learned to get along with other Earthlings. Many leaders want power for themselves. Many nations of the world are in competition with each other instead of being helpful to each other. Some leaders want to expand their territories and are willing to risk the lives of their own countrymen, sending them into battle to kill people of other nations, in order to fulfill their mad lust for power. It's not the people who want that; it's the leaders.

What's above is just something to be aware of.

At the first sign of unwarranted aggression on the part of a leader, at election time we should peacefully exercise our right to vote. The way to peace is to be peaceful, just as I wrote in my book *Zen and the Art of Happiness*: "There is only one way to achieve lasting happiness. That way is simply: Be happy." That may sound simplistic, I know, but it's true. The same is true about peace: The way to have peace is to be peaceful. (That does not mean nonaction. As Gandhi taught, "nonviolence is an active force of the highest order.")

Once again, keep in mind that the greatest honor one can have is simply to have been chosen to be part of the Taoverse. It doesn't matter if you're not smart, not good looking, not brave, not the most popular person in your crowd, not a great athlete, not a good student, not a good provider, or if you feel you haven't accomplished much in life. Neither does it matter if you've excelled in all of those things. Focus your attention on your greatest honor:

You have been chosen. That's a fact. To be part of the Taoverse. That's a fact. It's the greatest honor anyone can hold. And that, too, is a fact.

Those facts make you the equal of anyone. The goal is to maintain that awareness, to cultivate what Dermot Obrien so beautifully calls *"consciousness drained of doubt."*[©] One more fact: To fully enjoy the honor and to obtain favor from Tao, you need to be the kind of person . . . well, by this time you know who you need to be. And remember, who Tao has chosen to exist, you should not demean.

Tao created the Taoverse from Tao. Tao is all there was, is, or ever will be. Therefore, everything exists as and in Tao. And it's all alive. And that is the miracle.

> *You are never forgotten but at every moment are held in the great awareness. Open yourself to the possibilities inherent in your existence.*

Your Destiny

*"Our life is the result of
what we've set into motion. . . .
You are shaping your destiny
moment by moment."*

4

....

Your Destiny

We all have a destiny—and we all participate in shaping our destiny. Our destiny is not fixed. It's a moving destiny, one that we constantly influence and shape as we move along our path toward enlightenment. The manner in which I learned about destiny, time, and the future was probably the greatest and most profound gift the Taoverse could have bestowed upon me at that time in my life. I am still benefiting from it fifty-six years later and now you will also have the opportunity to benefit from it.

It was in 1966, after I had opened PHD (Prentiss-Hormel Development Company) on Malibu Beach with a partner, Tom Hormel. Tom was a good friend, an artist, a composer, and a businessman. The head of our art department,

Benita, an Austrian baroness, had gone to visit a fortune-teller in San Bernardino, and all she could talk about was how he could see into the future. She insisted I go. I told her I didn't believe in such things and I wouldn't go even if he was across the street. Benita pestered me for three months until one day I said, "Okay, Benita. I'll pick you up in the morning and we'll go."

It was a two-and-a-half-hour drive to this man's old wooden house on a dusty lot on the outskirts of San Bernardino. Parked in front of the house were several dozen cars. The governor of one of the Western states was there as well as a group of people waiting their turn. All the Beach Boys were inside waiting for a peek into their future. Mike Love and I talked the day away. The supposed fortune-teller, George Darius, spent five, ten, sometimes twenty minutes with each visitor.

My turn came late in the afternoon. George was in a tiny room with a desk and two chairs. There was one window high up toward the ceiling and the afternoon sun was shining through it. Benita had told me he would not let me record the conversation, but I could take notes. George was about five feet eight inches tall, a bit paunchy, and had a heavily lined face with jowls that hung down, pouches under his eyes, and wispy grey hair. He looked to be about ninety, but he was actually seventy-four.

George had false teeth top and bottom and they weren't glued in, so they clicked when he talked and it caused him to speak in a funny way. He asked where I was born. I told him. He asked when I was born. When I told him, he replied, "Oh, good day. Charlie Chaplin born on that day—good day."

He glanced up toward the window and suddenly looked at me with a surprised expression and said in a voice filled with excitement, "Oh! Oh! I wish I had your future! Up! Up! Always up!" George talked to me for two and a half hours. He kept everyone waiting. He told me of the events to come in my life. He said, "You're going to write books, lots of books." (This is my sixteenth book.) And he told me I would make movies. "But," he said, "the first movie you make, you'll neglect to sign a distribution agreement and the film will be shelved for ten years."

Seeing the Future

I had never thought about making a movie, but years later, in 1970, my son Todd and I wrote a story about a boy and a dog who traveled across America "lookin' for home." I liked the story and produced and directed the movie *Goin' Home* to subtly deliver a good message that home is where your heart is. I didn't know how to make a movie and it took me six years to finish it due to my ignorance and the fact that I regularly ran out of money. Rank Film Distributors in London was interested in distributing the film, and after I completed it they screened it at Pinewood Studios for three hundred employees of the Rank Group. The audience loved the film and they asked me to sign a contract with them to distribute it worldwide.

The next morning I sat in their office, contract in front of me, and I asked the managing director how much Rank would spend on TV advertising. He replied with a fine British accent, "We don't do that." I asked if TV advertising for a movie had *ever* been done in England. "No," he said. I was excited because in America that was being done with great success and I knew that the first few films they advertised on TV would produce blockbuster results. I wanted a TV campaign. They wouldn't budge. I wouldn't budge.

By that time, I knew that George could see the future because of many events he had told me about that had come to pass just as he said they would. Given what he had said about me *neglecting* to sign a distribution agreement, I had kept in the forefront of my mind that if I ever had the opportunity to sign a contract that I *wanted* to sign, I would not neglect to do so—because he had clearly said that I would *neglect* to sign a distribution agreement, not that I would *refuse* to sign it.

That distinction was very much in my mind as I sat there looking at the contract. After a lot of careful thought, George's words ringing in my ears, I refused to sign it. I made that decision because I realized that I was not *neglecting* an opportunity by not signing the contract; I was making a difficult but fully informed decision. If George had said during our first meeting that I would "refuse" to sign the agreement, I would have heeded that warning and been sure to sign the agreement. Perhaps he had assumed that I would fail to sign the agreement out of neglect. Yet it was his use of the word *neglect* that made the outcome he had seen possible.

I remained in England for six months attempting to raise the money to pay for TV advertising or to get Rank Distributors to change their minds, but to no avail. I went back to the U.S. to try and raise money for a TV campaign, but I got busy and here it is, forty-five years later, and the film has been sitting on the shelf all this time. However, I have now had *Goin' Home* transferred to Blu-ray Disc for viewing (see link at the back of the book).

From that experience and several others, I learned that George could not see numbers. He had said my first movie would be shelved "for ten years," but that just meant "a long time." So I learned to be careful in interpreting what George predicted when numbers were involved.

Once I knew George could actually see the future, I visited him regularly. His gift was accurate in everything but numbers. It was difficult to believe, yet over the years all that he saw for my life took place. I thought that it might be because I was participating in making it happen, but some of the things he saw were not in my control; they just happened.

So that you can understand how accurate George's vision was in seeing the future, I will relate one more instance. In 1968, I took Todd, who was then nine years old, to see George. He was only with George about two minutes. Surprised, I asked him what happened. He said, "George told me I would go to Hawaii and meet the girl of my dreams, the most important woman of my life."

"That's wonderful," I said. "Do you know how important that is? You know where to find the most important woman of your life." Todd waited twenty years to go to Hawaii. He was twenty-nine. I was excited for him. When he came back two weeks later, I asked, "Who is she?" He told me he hadn't met her. "No, that can't be," I said. "George is always right."

"He wasn't right this time," Todd responded. "The only interesting girl I met was a twenty-one-year-old bartender I talked with for a couple of hours one night." I said he should go to Hawaii again because George was always right.

Todd waited ten more years to go back. He was now thirty-nine. He had become a night-club owner and dated girls nearly every night, sometimes several on weekends. He had never been in love and never had a serious relationship. He didn't find the woman of his dreams on that trip either. Ten years later, when he was forty-nine, he again went back to Hawaii and again didn't find her. He told me he was not going to Hawaii anymore, that George was right about my future but not his.

A few years later, when he was fifty-three, Todd went to visit a friend who owned a little ranch in Topanga Canyon, California. His friend wasn't there, but his sister, Jill, was. It was late afternoon. They shared a beer and ended up spending the night together. Todd called me the next morning and said he was in love. I told him he was infatuated. "No," he said. "It's the real thing." The two became inseparable. They were together every day. He gave up seeing all other women.

After they had been together about six months, he and Jill were reminiscing one evening about their past and that was when they remembered each other: *Jill was the twenty-one-year-old bartender Todd had met the first time he went to Hawaii.* They just celebrated their ninth wedding anniversary and own a little ranch in

California. George saw Todd meeting Jill in Hawaii and her importance in his life when Todd was nine years old.

George could see the future as well as the past. Time was not a barrier for him. He could see forward or backward in time. I do not know if George could see the future when someone was not in his presence, but he could certainly see it when someone was there with him. To be clear, I'm not saying that our future is 100 percent predestined.

> *Our destiny does exist, but we also participate in creating it. You change your future and influence it by how you are being every moment.*

Time, Change, and the Eternally Present Now

I have learned much about our universe from the things George saw. You can, too, from reading this. What I take away from my experiences with George is that the past, the present, and the future all exist in the same time. For the events of the past, present, and future to all exist at once, "time" is necessary. George could see the future and the past because they exist in time.

Time makes existence possible. Existence occurs in time. Time has always existed—as Tao's eternal consciousness.

The definition of now: Tao's eternal presence.
We live, we exist, within Tao—within Tao's
consciousness.

As we've already talked about, time did not begin with the Big Bang. The Big Bang was just a minor incident in an ever-present now.

Perhaps it seems to you as if time flows to you from the future, actually bringing your future, creating your now, passing beyond you and creating your past, and that you participate by interacting with what is happening around you—aging, experiencing a flowing of events and changes, and interacting with them as time moves past you. The great misunderstanding about time is the belief that time moves—the future becoming the present, the present becoming the past. It's not like that.

Time does not move. Change creates the impression, the experience, of time moving. But time itself does not move. We live in an eternal now *in which change occurs.*

Everything that was created changes. But time was not created. Time does not change. Time does not "do" anything. *Time* is a word we use to describe what existence exists in.

There are three kinds of change: cyclical change, where the change reoccurs, as in the four seasons; sequential change, which goes on forever; and nonchange, which is the background against which change becomes perceptible. In existence, there are three different stages of change: before, during, and after. "During" is "now." But it's only because *you* are in the picture that before, during, and after exist. Without you, existence just is.

To say it another way, eternity (time) goes backward and forward only from your vantage point, from your perspective. If you weren't in the picture, eternity would just be. Only "now" exists—no future, no past. Endless time *is*.

The past, present, and future all exist within an eternal now.

Did you ever wonder what the world would look like if you weren't there to experience it—

if you could "step out" of time and look in on it? And where your vantage point would be? Since past and future exist at the same time, and only "now" exists for you, could you look in at any point in "time"?

Your Constantly Changing Destiny

We each have a destiny and, as you have seen, some people can see destinies. Now for the important question: *Who or what created your destiny?*

Simple. You and Tao did. Tao created your primary destiny from the time of the Big Bang, billions of years before we were Homo sapiens. You changed your original destiny by how you were being during all of your lifetimes, all your incarnations, even as you are doing now.

Your destiny is constantly changing according to your actions. We create our future by how we are being at every moment. Through the use of free will, we change our destiny. Not completely— the earthquake will still come as will the other events in your life. But as an evolved being, the effects of those events will be lessened. Or as an unevolved being, they won't be.

We don't create all of our future because our planet itself has a future and the human race has a future. If it is the future of our planet to be drawn into a black hole, we will all go with it. (Again, as I said in chapter 3, you would just transition.) But if it is our planet's future to gloriously exist, within that future we can and do influence our own future. Some of us influence it consciously, some not. You can be one who creates your future consciously. *You are the author of every next moment.*

Open yourself just for this moment to consider that this is true: *I have been a participant in creating my destiny—past, present, and future . . . always.* You can always return to your former belief, whatever that was, but for this little bit of time allow yourself to consider that it's true that you are a participant in creating your destiny and see how that resonates with you.

Your destiny was billions of years in the making. Approximately four billion years ago, in one of your earliest life-forms, you were living in the ocean in a hydrothermal vent as a microorganism. That was your ancestor.

The Paleozoic time spanned from roughly 541 million years ago to 252 million years ago and is subdivided into six geologic periods. From oldest to youngest they are Cambrian, Ordovician, Silurian, Devonian, Carboniferous, and Permian. Life was present in all of them, *your life.* That's because life, from its earliest forms, reincarnated, evolved, or morphed (changed smoothly from one form to another). But it was always going to be you at this time. Each evolutionary life you lived added to your destiny.

It took 4.5 billion years for our Tao to prepare earth for you. And it was more than just for you. There are more than 7.8 billion of us here now and more coming. Those who came, finished their time here on earth, and transitioned number roughly 108 billion. If you have never ordered a report on your ancestry, I recommend it. It's not expensive and will reveal enormous amounts of information about your ancestors going back to caveman days. It will help solidify who you were then and who you are now. It may also trigger some memories of past lives.

*We are old, very old. We are also new, very new.
We are as old as our first incarnation and we
are as new as this moment.*

There never was a time when you weren't.
There will never be a time when you aren't. There
is nothing in the Taoverse more the Taoverse than
you. You always were. You will always be.

Survivors All

If we traveled far enough back in time, we would
discover that we shared common ancestors with
every other living organism. That is an essential bit
of information. We share DNA with every species of plant and animal. In addition to that, you
are the child of survivors. More than 99 percent
of all life-forms that existed on planet Earth are
gone, extinct, but your ancestors survived—all of
them. They survived long enough to give birth to
another of your ancestors.

Going back billions of years, in an unbroken
line of succession, through hundreds of thousands
of lifetimes, all your ancestors were survivors. You,

at this moment, except for any children you may have, are the latest survivor of your ancestors. Every life-form that ever existed that gave birth to another of its kind was a survivor. They survived every kind of catastrophe, including the five ice ages in Earth's history: Huronian, Cryogenian, Andean-Saharan, late Paleozoic, and the current one, the Quaternary Ice Age (we are in-between ice ages).

Your direct ancestors of the hominin family, including the great apes, honed their skills for millions of years—toughing it out, fighting for survival, warding off every kind of danger, killing when the need arose, overcoming every obstacle, being protected from birth until they could fend for themselves and live long enough to produce an offspring that, after millions of years, became you—life after life, form after form, death after death.

And now . . . *you're here.*

In all the forms that preceded you, your ancestors developed the intelligence, courage, wisdom, craftiness, strength, brutality, daring, and imagination to survive until they produced an offspring. Billions of years of gradual development, through the eons, have gone into the creation of you.

Can you imagine what powerful qualities are inherent in your DNA? What reserves you actually possess? What skills, what strength, what ingenuity, what courage, and what resourcefulness all lie within you, waiting to be called upon?

Every one of your ancestors in every life and in every form was a winner in that they survived long enough to produce another of your ancestors.

Now that you know who you are and who your ancestors were and what qualities you possess, you can go forth and live what's remaining to you of this lifetime with a new awareness, not only of who you are and who you were but where you came from and from whom: *survivors all*. Think of that the next time you want to accomplish something, the next time you are faced with adversity or a difficulty, an obstacle or a problem.

Call upon that which is in you. It is truly who you are. Let that be your new awareness.

Here's a little something to lighten this up from the poet Langdon Smith (1858-1908).

Evolution

When you were a tadpole and I was a fish
  In the Paleozoic time,
And side by side on the ebbing tide
  We sprawled through the ooze and slime,
Or skittered with many a caudal flip
  Through the depths of the Cambrian fen,
My heart was rife with the joy of life,
  For I loved you even then.

Mindless we lived and mindless we loved
  And mindless at last we died;
And deep in the rift of the Caradoc drift
  We slumbered side by side.
The world turned on in the lathe of time,
  The hot lands heaved amain,
Till we caught our breath from the womb of death
  And crept into life again.

We were amphibians, scaled and tailed,
  And drab as a dead man's hand;
We coiled at ease 'neath the dripping trees
  Or trailed through the mud and sand.
Croaking and blind, with our three-clawed feet

Writing a language dumb,
With never a spark in the empty dark
  To hint at a life to come.

Yet happy we lived and happy we loved,
  And happy we died once more;
Our forms were rolled in the clinging mold
  Of a Neocomian shore.
The eons came and the eons fled
  And the sleep that wrapped us fast
Was riven away in a newer day
  And the night of death was passed.

Then light and swift through the jungle trees
  We swung in our airy flights,
Or breathed in the balms of the fronded palms
  In the hush of the moonless nights;
And oh! what beautiful years were there
  When our hearts clung each to each;
When life was filled and our senses thrilled
  In the first faint dawn of speech.

Thus life by life and love by love
  We passed through the cycles strange,
And breath by breath and death by death

We followed the chain of change.
Till there came a time in the law of life
  When over the nursing sod
The shadows broke and the soul awoke
  In a strange, dim dream of God.

I was thewed like an Auroch bull
  And tusked like the great cave bear;
And you, my sweet, from head to feet
  Were gowned in your glorious hair.
Deep in the gloom of a fireless cave,
  When the night fell o'er the plain
And the moon hung red o'er the river bed
  We mumbled the bones of the slain.

I flaked a flint to a cutting edge
  And shaped it with brutish craft;
I broke a shank from the woodland lank
  And fitted it, head and haft;
Than I hid me close to the reedy tarn,
  Where the mammoth came to drink;
Through the brawn and bone I drove the stone
  And slew him upon the brink.

Loud I howled through the moonlit wastes,
  Loud answered our kith and kin;
From west to east to the crimson feast
  The clan came tramping in.
O'er joint and gristle and padded hoof
  We fought and clawed and tore,
And cheek by jowl with many a growl
  We talked the marvel o'er.

I carved that fight on a reindeer bone
  With rude and hairy hand;
I pictured his fall on the cavern wall
  That men might understand.
For we lived by blood and the right of might
  Ere human laws were drawn,
And the age of sin did not begin
  Till our brutal tusks were gone.

And that was a million years ago
  In a time that no man knows;
Yet here tonight in the mellow light
  We sit at Delmonico's.
Your eyes are deep as the Devon springs,
  Your hair is dark as jet,

Your years are few, your life is new,
  Your soul untried, and yet—

Our trail is on the Kimmeridge clay
  And the scarp of the Purbeck flags;
We have left our bones in the Bagshot stones
  And deep in the Coralline crags;
Our love is old, our lives are old,
  And death shall come amain;
Should it come today, what man may say
  We shall not live again?

God wrought our souls from the Tremadoc beds
  And furnish'd them wings to fly;
He sowed our spawn in the world's dim dawn,
  And I know that it shall not die,
Though cities have sprung above the graves
  Where the crook-bone men made war
And the ox-wain creaks o'er the buried caves
  Where the mummied mammoths are.

Then as we linger at luncheon here
  O'er many a dainty dish,
Let us drink anew to the time when you
  Were a tadpole and I was a fish.

So here we are, Tao's latest incarnation of the species hominin on planet Earth. Hurray for us! Hurray for you! You were billions of years in the making. And no matter what comes next, *you'll be there* . . . in one way, shape, form or another. *And that is the miracle.*

Karma, Intention, and Destiny

As you lived through each of your forms, your destiny has changed according to your actions and beliefs. Events and your response to them changed your destiny in accordance with what you intended by your actions. If you hurt someone unintentionally, it did not cause an adverse reaction to your karmic destiny. If you hurt someone intentionally, you changed your karmic destiny. If you were mean to someone, your karmic destiny changed to take into account what your meanness would create in your life and in the life of the person you were mean to—a constantly moving, shifting panorama of destinies. That is what I mean when I say that you create your destiny moment by moment as you are *being* at every moment.

All the changes in your life that have occurred

and will continue to occur are governed by Tao's laws. We humans break human laws regularly. Taoversal laws, natural laws, cannot be broken. You may have heard it said that if you break a law of nature, you must pay a price—perhaps getting fat from eating too much. In cases like that, you have not broken a law of nature; you were governed by it.

Karma is Tao's response to the sum of your actions. The most important information to know about karma is you create it.

When you become aware of that, you'll be very careful with your every act, knowing that you are creating karma, your destiny. Tao created a destiny for planet Earth. We fit ourselves into that destiny in the best way we know how. While being subject to the unfolding destiny of planet Earth and its inhabitants, we want to live happy, peaceful, and fulfilling lives.

Everyone creates karma—some with awareness, others without. And karma *always* fulfills itself, sometimes coming back to you immediately and sometimes spanning lifetimes.

Remember when we talked about Newton's

laws of motion? His third law of motion: *For every action, there is an equal and opposite reaction.* You can picture Newton's third law of action and reaction as what takes place when a tiny pebble is dropped into the water, creating a reaction that is in exact response to its size, weight, outer texture, shape, and velocity. Said another way, every action produces a reaction, and the reaction is in exact response to the action that produced it.

You may wonder why some of us live such pain-filled, terror-filled, miserable lives. Why some of us are born deformed or why we become disease-ridden or crippled or mentally disordered. Or why some of us, perhaps you, suffer. It's because our life is the result of what we've set into motion, not just in this one lifetime but in many lifetimes.

Every action of any kind, including words, thoughts, feelings, and the totality of your existence, will cause a reaction that will be in exact response to whatever produced it, sooner or later, even if that spans many lifetimes. Sometimes, of course, minor actions create major responses that seem not to be in accord with the action that created the response, such as when you knock over one domino and that one domino, falling, knocks down a line of dominoes. Or when the final weight of the last orange put in the wagon breaks the wagon's axle. Cases like that are often the cumulative result of what we've set in motion over a long time.

Yet here's something wonderful about karma. Let's say in a previous lifetime you were a nasty, evil person who created pain and misery for your fellow humans. Let's say in this lifetime, through thoughtful discovery and effort, you realized that you wanted to be a good person, bringing benefits to your fellow humans, and you lived your life in that manner. The karma from the past lifetime will come back and you will experience the karmic response, but because you are a different person, a good person benefiting others, the response you receive will be softer.

That also applies to karma you create in this lifetime. If you have been a bad person and mend your ways and become a good person, the karma you experience in this lifetime or your next lifetime will be softened. That's because *you are not the same person*. There is no point in correcting an already reformed person.

Every cause produces an effect, and the effect is in exact accord with the cause that produced it.

Even as we cannot escape our misdeeds of this lifetime or past lifetimes, neither can we lose the blessings of earlier lifetimes as we stretched ourselves to goodness, to greatness. If our actions are the result of our intentions and our intentions are to do good, create harmony, deal fairly, love dearly, and live the life of an enlightened person, as a result of natural law can anything happen except that we reach the loftiest goals to which one can attain and lead lives of greatest happiness?

The Real Law of Evolution

We are on this earth to learn, and we are each other's sharpening stone. Remember:

Tao's favorite tool is adversity. The karma and adversity we experience is only for guidance.

We are here to evolve into perfect humans. That's what evolution is. We are always trending toward a more perfect expression of human.

The law of evolution provides that everything

in our created Taoverse is trending toward a more perfect model of itself. Plants and animals constantly evolve toward a greater ability to survive in their circumstances. If our global climate warms, in a few decades polar bears will have short hair. Each new generation is, for the most part, smarter than the previous generation. Because of the law of evolution, your goal as a human is to achieve the status of "Ultimate Human." That's part of Tao's intention for us all.

Because we are a part of Tao and because of the law of evolution, *we always win*, even though it may take lifetimes. I also talk about this in my tiny book *God's Game*. I invite you to read it for free or listen to it (see the link at the back of this book).

In our Taoverse, there is only winning. However, if you are not living as an enlightened person, as an ambassador of Tao, your present condition and circumstances may feel like losing. But that's because you may be living your life partly as an unjust person or a person who takes advantage of others or a person who may be ungrateful, mean, thoughtless, uncaring, revengeful, perhaps a hoarder bent only on selfish gratification.

You may also feel as if you are losing because you have not yet fully accepted one of the fundamental truths I introduced at the beginning of this book—that everything happens for a reason and the reason is so you can be benefited, which we'll explore in detail in the next chapter. It could also be due to karma at work from a previous lifetime. But even if that's the case, as I said, you can soften the karmic response that is coming back to you by changing into a better version of yourself. If you have not been living in accord with what is highest and best within you, as you progress through the knowings you can change that.

We may not reach our goal of becoming a perfect human being in this lifetime, but *we have many lifetimes and eternity within which to evolve.* And we will ultimately achieve our goal.

If, due to the circumstances of your life, you have lived or are living an unhappy life, you may not want to come back to earth to live again; but that's not in your control. You may have heard that the goal of Shakyamuni, the Buddha, also known as Siddhartha Gautama, was to end his cycle of birth and rebirth. He may have achieved that, but I believe it is unlikely as there is always more to learn. There's a test you can use to see if there's more for you to learn: *If you're alive, there's more.*

You may have forgotten how you came to earth, but you know the way. And what you have done once, you can do again and probably have done in many prior lifetimes.

In all your forms, the consciousness that inhabited your body—that was you. That is you now.

Tao's consciousness has always existed. It will always exist—no beginning, no end. You have always existed and will always exist—forming, unforming, re-forming. An exquisite panorama of change, all alive, all conscious, all aware, and all *you. And that is the miracle.*

We cannot conceive of something that has always existed, something without a beginning or an ending. That's because we live in a world of seeming beginnings and seeming endings, even though there are no real beginnings or endings. Everything is just a flow of events, conditions, situations, and physical manifestations that are in constant motion, constant change, seeming to exist and then to no longer exist as they flow into their next evolutionary form.

The dinosaurs were on earth for roughly 165 million years. They became extinct about 65 million years ago. Spiders have been here 350 million years. Even in one of our earliest hominid forms, Ardipithecus kadabba, we've only been here less than 6 million years. In relation to the dinosaurs and spiders, *we've just begun*. As humans, we're in our infancy.

Transitions

The early Egyptians were among the first to believe in alchemy, the forerunner of modern chemistry, based on the transformation of matter. They were attempting to convert base metals into gold or to find an elixir, a substance, that would prolong life indefinitely and would cure all illnesses. They believed if they could reduce matter to its purest form, it would become gold or could be transformed into the aforesaid elixir. They failed.

For myself, I do not want to live this lifetime forever, alluring as that may seem. That would ultimately be boring, no matter how good it would be. Besides, I'm looking forward to the next phase with the anticipation that it will be wonderful, being liberated from my body, remaining as pure consciousness.

When I'm old and my body ages and I can't run and jump and move easily, I'll be happy to move on *as my consciousness* in my new ethereal body—a new, vibrant energy form with new challenges and new experiences, preparing to come back to earth again

Even if my body didn't wear out, I'd still like this incarnation to end after a certain length of time. Since evolution only moves in one direction, I'll have a better body and a better brain but with the same mind. I will take the same mind with me into the next realm because that *is* me—not the three pounds of fat and water that's stored in the top third of my skull, but the intelligence that uses it to function in the physical realm. The same is true for you.

Here is another Taoversal law that applies to seeming death. For something to become hot, it must first be cold. For something to become cold, it must first be hot. For something to become light, it must first be dark. For something to become dark, it must first be light. For something to become fast, it must first be slow. For something to become slow, it must first be fast.

For something to become dead, it must first be alive. For something to become alive, it must first be dead—not "dead" in the sense of "disappear from the Taoverse." That is not possible, as nothing can actually die or disappear from the Taoverse. The physical part of us changes form as it decomposes, but your essence, your consciousness, will have the same form as when you were temporarily using your body as a place in which to live. It will be made of a different substance, an ethereal substance. It will closely resemble you but without blemish or fault.

As you transition at the end of this life, your physical body will begin its slow transformation into the substances that will support other living things. Your consciousness, however, will not transform. It is already a complete entity unto itself. Your consciousness is your spirit, and it is always total, whole, impervious, luminescent, and pure. It is still subject to Tao's laws, although those laws are different from the laws we experience as humans.

You, as pure consciousness, are temporarily residing in your body.

Your consciousness and your body, along with everything else in the Taoverse, live within the ether that is Tao. Tao is endless life. Since both your body and your consciousness are already in Tao's ether, you, as pure consciousness, continue to live on in Tao's ether.

Therefore, when your time to leave your body arrives, it is only transition at work, a release of consciousness from the body you used for a while to experience life on earth in order to learn, to progress, to evolve, to become enlightened as to who you really are, and then to live successive lives accordingly as a *conscious ambassador of Tao*—or not.

At the moment after transition, you are aware of all of your previous incarnations in which you had awareness. All the entities that were "you" that have manifested over thousands of years are present within your awareness. You must review them to see what progress or lack of it you accomplished in the incarnation just past. (When we reincarnate, we will most likely not retain the memories of the incarnation we're in now, although some people do have the gift of being able to see events from past lives.)

The Chinese masters who lived thousands of

years ago who knew of Tao and its ways said there are dark spirits and light spirits. They said that when it is time for spirits to transition, the light spirits, after a brief time, may reincarnate. The dark spirits experience a more intensive review of their past lifetime so that they can learn from it, and then they, too, may reincarnate.

Thus, after every lifetime, those who lived according to the laws of Tao can promptly live another time on earth. We return here to learn, to experience, but because of our prior lifetime's exemplary behavior, we may, in our own unique way, become a teacher to others, a healer, or a powerful person who sets an example for others in being an ambassador of Tao.

In every lifetime, we choose to gravitate toward the light or the dark. As we continue to choose to evolve toward the light, it becomes part of our nature and we naturally develop an inclination to gravitate toward the light—so much so that when we digress from the path of light, or even when a thought arises to digress from the light, an uneasy feeling comes over us.

It is *so* exhilarating to live in the light. It's like standing in warm sunshine on a cold day.

Our Eternal Spirit
and Our Brand-New Existence

During the time I was writing this book, I had my first experience of "living" inside my eighty-four-year-old body. I experienced this as I was getting out of a deep armchair after an hour of watching a film. As I struggled to get up, I was not the eighty-four-year-old Chris. I was a much younger entity, a vital entity, using my body to get up. It was a distinct feeling, a clear, powerful experience. I had been writing about our bodies not being "us" for the past couple of years, but at that moment I experienced it. I was completely aware that "I" was not my body, that I was an eternal spirit using my body to get out of the chair.

Late in the evening of the next day, I read to my wife, Lyn, what I have written here about that experience. I told her that the part of me that was reading to her was not the physical part of me, that I still had the sensation of being the "me" that is living in my body. Ever-practical Lyn said, "Okay, it's time for you to bring your physical self to bed."

As you continue to evolve and live your life, applying what you are learning here, keep in mind that you are shaping your destiny moment by moment. Look at your life from the perspective of Tao. Recall these truths that we talked about in our conversation on destiny, karma, and transition . . .

The Taoverse is perfect. It was created perfect and remains perfect through an eternity of constant change, an endless past and an endless future—unbroken, already created perfection in which you participate by being Who You Are at every moment, endlessly. *And that is the miracle.*

Our life goes on being perfect as time seemingly reveals itself moment by moment. It may seem as if you are standing in a river of time, with the future coming toward you and the past unrolling behind—that where you are standing is a tiny hairline of time we call "now" that separates the future from the past. However, all that exists is an eternal now in which endless change takes place.

Our Big Bang is old, fourteen thousand million years old. Our Big Bang is new, as new as the next moment in time. *A totally new existence every moment, always, in all ways.*

Our Taoverse and everything in it is in a constant state of change. Our entire Taoverse, down to its tiniest particle, moves and changes instantly, constantly. Therefore, our Taoverse is brand-new every instant—as new as the first instant of the Big Bang. There is no instant of time when our existence is not brand-new.

When our Big Bang blew into existence, it was just a ripple in time. It wasn't there . . . and then it was there. What is so vitally important to us is *it happened*. And when it happened, the conditions were set in motion for *us* to happen, and it was all brand-new. Every instant. And as it was instantly, constantly changing, it was—and still is—a brand-new existence.

Every time you blink your eyes, when you open them it's a brand-new Taoverse—all of it, even to its tiniest particle.

Think what that means to you, the opportunities it makes available. A brand-new Taoverse *every moment*—one that you can co-create.

Knowing all that, create your destiny consciously—with the awareness that you *are* creating your destiny. Having that potential is the miracle.

Living an
Authentic Life

"We must each walk our own path to enlightenment. That is the way."

道

5

....

Living an Authentic Life

Twenty-five hundred years ago, the sage Lao Tzu, meaning "Old Master" (his original name was Li Er), was known throughout China as the greatest master of living in harmony with Tao. He was a famous philosopher and teacher who had devoted his life to following the principles of Tao. In his later years, Lao Tzu (pronounced "Lao T'sa") was keeper of the archives in Loyang, an ancient capital of China. He had always refused to write down what he taught to prevent it from becoming an empty dogma that people would follow rather than discovering Tao for themselves.

As he neared the end of his life, disenchanted with the people for not following the simple yet profound ways of Tao, Lao Tzu mounted a water buffalo and, with his beloved disciple leading it along, rode off hundreds of miles, intending to leave China forever. The man in charge of the last outpost, some say an old friend and devoted follower of Lao Tzu and Tao, pleaded with him to write what he knew of Tao so that the great wisdom would be preserved and his teachings would not become misinterpreted and corrupted.

Lao Tzu stayed and wrote the eighty-one verses that have become known as the Tao Te Ching, which, again, literally means "The Book of the Way (Tao) and Its Virtue (Te)" or, as one well-known version calls it, "The Way of Life." Once Lao Tzu completed his task, he sent his disciple home and rode off into the wilderness, never to be seen or heard of again.

The picture you see here is a painting of Lao Tzu leaving Loyang to go into the wilderness. It was given to me thirty years ago by Jonathan Jiang, a highly skilled acupuncturist and massage therapist from China who practices in Los Angeles. We became good friends and he gave me the picture because of my great interest in Lao Tzu's philosophy. At the time Jonathan gave me the painting, we didn't know that it was so you could see it now.

I recommend you read Lao Tzu's book. My favorite translation is that of Witter Bynner. The themes you've been reading about in this book are also found in that wonderful classic. For example, the Tao Te Ching describes Tao as the mother and the ancestor of all things—the unchangeable that existed "before heaven and earth." It says Tao is a treasure and a refuge that turns no one away. All things depend on Tao, while Tao depends on nothing.

The Tao Te Ching also describes the attributes of "the sage," whom all of us can aspire to become. To Lao Tzu, the sage is the ideal human being, the person who is one with the laws of nature, one with Tao. The sages are the ones I refer to as "enlightened."

We are all on the way to becoming enlightened.

It may take us many lifetimes, but we all are on our way. The Tao Te Ching points us to the path of authentic living and shows us how to live in harmony with Tao and thrive while on our path toward enlightenment.

Living an authentic life means living your life being true to what is highest and best within you without misrepresentation. Doing so, your life will be forever better, more real.

Living authentically is living as the real you without deception. It means you are the person you say you are, not the person you want people to believe you are or the person others expect you to be. No exaggerations. No false images or claims. When you boast or exaggerate, it is due to a feeling of inadequacy. The ancient Chinese had a saying for it: "Better to go on foot than to ride in a carriage under false pretenses."

Living authentically is living in harmony with your true nature, according to the principles of Tao—living with the awareness that you are a golden child of an aware, conscious Taoverse of which you are an inseparable part and that you should therefore act accordingly.

Walking Your Own Path

Lao Tzu, along with all the great sages, knew this truth about the path to enlightenment: every plan you ever make has only one constant—you. Not that you are always the same, but that you are always part of your plan. All else may come and go as the plan unfolds—friends, parents, possessions, conditions, situations, finances, and associates. You are the only *certain* constant.

Therefore, to be successful in any plan, you must be able to depend on yourself for strength, honor, endurance, capability, justice, righteousness, imagination, truthfulness, resourcefulness, trustworthiness, determination, and courage. If you are lacking in any of those areas of character, any plan you make will be flawed. So if your plan fails, do not look outside of yourself for the cause—look within. It is within that you will find the flaw. Know yourself. As the Tao Te Ching famously advises: "He who knows others is wise; / He who knows himself is enlightened."[1]

Although we all live in the same Taoverse, each of us, in effect, lives in a different Taoverse. The difference is caused by our individual perception of the Taoverse in which we reside and by what we believe to be true about the Taoverse and about life and how to live it.

Standing around the perimeter of a pond with the moon shining on the water, everyone points to a different place on the water where they see the moon's reflection. Ten different people can experience or view an event and all ten may give a different report of it. Some people have good vision, others do not. The Taoverse perceived by those with poor vision is different than the Taoverse perceived by a person with good vision.

Likewise, each person has a different belief about people, events, conditions, fate, existence, God or gods, and what it all means. Thus, each of us lives in a different world according to our beliefs and perceptions. What binds us together is that we are all subject to the same Taoversal laws and *we all exist in Tao*.

Just as we all perceive the world differently, it is also true that the path each of us walks is unique.

> *The path that one person follows is not*
> *the correct path for any other person.*
> *We must each walk our own path to*
> *enlightenment. That is the way.*

Know, too, that what we desire, what we work for, and what we seek after are not the ultimate goals. They are the merely the objects that lead us on the path where our life unfolds. It is the path *itself* where we experience life and where we obtain the wisdom and knowledge of the Taoverse. To walk the path with the awareness that you are a child of the Taoverse, that you have a purpose being here, that you have lived before and will live again, and that whatever befalls you on your path is for your ultimate good—that is how to live with the awareness that brings abundant, joyful life and is in keeping with "what is."

It's Perfect

I said earlier that the Taoverse is perfect, that it remains perfect through an eternity of constant change, and that you participate in this already created perfection by being Who You Are at every moment. What does that mean for you? It means that when an event occurs, it's perfect . . . even though it may not appear to be.

Our Taoverse would be in danger of its own destruction if an imperfect event could occur. One imperfect event could lead to two, three, and more, leading to destruction. But that doesn't happen. Our Taoverse is always perfect, an unbroken stream of perfection that persists into eternity. Even if our galaxy were to be suddenly drawn into a magnificent black hole, it would still be part of the perfection of All-That-Is. We are also part of *that*.

There is one more aspect to the concept that all events are perfect. You have heard it said that "everything happens for a reason." But have you ever heard anyone say what the reason is?

Everything happens for a reason, and the reason is so you can be benefited.

It might be hard for you to believe that the loss of the favorite watch your best friend gave you, the banged toe, the torn clothing, the car accident, the lost wallet or purse, the grave misunderstanding, the relationship breakup, the cancer verdict, or the shrinking bank account or portfolio are completely beneficial for you, but that is why there are so few people who are truly happy and have life the way they want it.

Being happy requires practice. As long as you treat seemingly bad things as though they are truly bad, you give them the power to be bad.

This concept is a bit like serendipity, a wonderful word that comes from a tale about the three princes of Serendip (Sri Lanka), who had gone off at the request of their father, the king, to experience life away from the palace. They traveled for years and had many experiences. Some seemed fortunate and some seemed very unfortunate.

As the English writer Horace Walpole, who first coined the term *serendipity,* said, "As their highnesses travelled, they were always making discoveries," accidentally and through their own discerning insight, "of things which they were not in quest of." Serendipity, then, means accidentally or unintentionally finding something that is fortunate or valuable—even if it comes in the form of adversity. It is through misfortune that we experience that gifts can flow to us.

There is nothing in our Taoverse more our Taoverse than you are. You are cared for and cherished. If you have not felt that you are being cared for and benefited, it is probably because you are not fully aware of Tao's favorite tool for endlessly shaping us: *adversity.* We touched on this earlier.

Without adversity, there would be no need for effort and hardly any growth—spiritual, mental, or physical. Every day a cool, easy trip to the mall, the tennis court, the pool, the bank, the grocery store, and the health club. Every plan working out. Constant success. In contrast, times of challenge require great effort just to keep on an even keel, and even that is sometimes not enough. Adversity, then, calls forth your best effort and keeps you alert and moving forward on your path—all of which bring you great benefits.

I know that everything that has happened to me has benefited me, so I have no remorse in my life. No "if only I hadn't done that" or "why did that nasty accident happen to me?" For me it's *all* perfect. A perfect life brought to me by perfect Tao.

That, I know, is difficult to accept, especially considering the disappointing events you've experienced—the ones you believed to be unfortunate, not to mention the big ones you believed to be devastating. But by treating those events as they *appeared* to you, you gave them the power to *be* unfortunate, even devastating. You suffered, not realizing that the events were part of the plan to give you strength, wisdom, and good fortune.

What you are discovering here is the way the Taoverse works. Here is the heart of it: We *are* the Taoverse. Tao does not hurt itself (remember, you are itself) without a purpose, which is to bring itself (you) a benefit. The truth is that every good thing, every wonderful thing, all the special things you experienced since those seemingly unfortunate events have been a direct result of those previous events—the ones that seemed unfortunate, even devastating. An unbroken chain of perfect events.

Something else to be mindful of is that Tao

provided every characteristic we have. Anger, hate, jealousy, greed, love, passion, disgust, anxiety, sadness, heartbreak, joy, exultation, awe, pity, hope, despair, enthusiasm, desire, shame, fear, envy? *Yes!* Every one of the characteristics has its opposite. How else would you be able to recognize happy unless you had experienced unhappiness, or cold unless you had experienced warm? Whatever exists in our Taoverse, seemingly good or seemingly bad, you can be certain Tao created it and had a purpose for it, a purpose to benefit us.

How We Respond to Events

An event is just an event. How you respond to the event determines its outcome in your life. Think of it like this. A train is coming down the track to the moment of the event. You're like the railroad switch. *Now* the event happens. *Now* you get to choose your response: positive or negative. You can either respond as if the event is terribly bad for you or wonderful for you. Your choice.

Everyone, including you, has experienced events that seemed horribly negative yet turned out to be wonderfully beneficial. Your very existence depended upon the occurrence of those seemingly negative experiences. You may think that's extreme—one of my bold statements—but that's how the Taoverse in which you live works.

Think of the countless hours you have spent in remorse, anger, frustration, and misery that you could have avoided had you been aware of the universal law that decreed that "from the first moment, what you experienced that seemed devastating was for your complete benefit."

I wrote about that in *Zen and the Art of Happiness,* where I ask you to imagine that God has just appeared before you and said, "I promise you that everything that happens to you from this moment forward will be of the greatest benefit to you and will bring you the utmost good fortune." Suppose God went on to say: "Even though what happens will sometimes appear unfortunate or hurtful, in the end your life will be wonderfully blessed and hugely benefited by *whatever* happens."

How would you feel about that news? Happy? Perhaps even joyful? Wouldn't it be the best piece of news you could possibly hear? Wouldn't you heave a deep sigh of relief and feel as if a great burden had been lifted from your shoulders?

If you didn't enthusiastically answer *yes*, perhaps you have mistaken what I am talking about. I am not talking about the phrase we commonly hear, "Try to make the best of it," which means "the situation or event really *is* bad and terribly unlucky, but do what you can to salvage some good out of it." Nor do I mean that within even the worst event possible, there can be found a tiny bit of good.

I am not thinking in terms of such limiting ideas. I am thinking in unlimited terms, where every event that befalls you is absolutely the best possible event that could occur—that there is no other event imaginable that could benefit you to any greater degree.

So, again, wouldn't that be the best piece of news you could hear? Wouldn't you heave a deep sigh of relief? And wouldn't you then respond to the next thing that happened—even if it was hurtful or took something or someone from you or seemed bad or unlucky—as though it was the best thing that could have happened?

From one of my favorite books, *The Rubaiyat*

of Omar Khayyam (1048-1131), translated by the poet and author Edward FitzGerald:

> Ah, Love! could you and I with Fate conspire
> To grasp this sorry Scheme of Things entire,
> Would not we shatter it to bits—and then
> Re-mold it nearer to the Heart's Desire!

As we cannot do what Omar suggests, if you are willing to give this new concept a chance and to actually believe and act on the basis that everything that happens to you is the best thing that could possibly happen to you, you will start to act in accord with that belief and, as a result of natural law, bring about that end. I'm suggesting that you "shatter to bits" your old limiting beliefs and take on a new belief that has the power to remold your life "nearer to your heart's desire."

Remember that for the fourteen thousand million years since our Big Bang, everything that happened in our cosmos must have been perfect for its continuance *given that it still exists.* That means whatever occurred must have benefited its continuation *in every way.* Our Taoverse is still unfolding exactly like that. Believe it. And what's more, you are part of "every way." That Taoversal law includes you. It is because of Tao's law of favorability that we are able to bring about the fruition of our plans.

> *So everything that has happened to you, that will happen to you, that is happening to you is perfect for you. Treat it that way and your whole existence will change—perfectly.*

You'll never know until you do.

The Power of a Strong Personal Philosophy

To show you how powerful these concepts are, let me give you some examples. I've learned first-hand how good things can emerge from even the hardest of times by maintaining a strong personal philosophy. Some of you may have read this story in more detail in my other books, but for those of you who haven't, I will share it briefly here.

When my son Pax was fifteen, he began using drugs and alcohol. When he was eighteen, he came home from school one day, began crying, and told me he was hooked on heroin. For the next six years, I battled heroin for Pax's life. We tried thirty-day, sixty-day, and ninety-day programs as well as addiction specialists, drug and alcohol therapists, and counselors of every sort. Nothing worked.

Finally, we put together our own holistic, hand-tailored program for recovery, which saved Pax's life. In 2001, Pax and I went on to found and codirect the first non-twelve-step drug-and-alcohol treatment center in the United States, Passages Addiction Cure Center in Malibu, to help others find their freedom. Today Pax is CEO of Passages and is running it masterfully and with great dedication. He's healthy, happy, prosperous, clear-minded, and cured—and helping others achieve the same freedom that he has achieved.

To some, Pax's years of addiction and trauma may seem like an irretrievable loss. Yet, if you were to ask Pax how he sees the years of his addiction—the beatings from drug dealers, the degradation, the loss of friends, respect, and his college years as well as his several near brushes with death—he would tell you that it was the most terrible experience of his life, and also the greatest. He would tell you that those years led him to his life's work, that without them he would never have had the idea or the drive to create Passages, and that he was being prepared for a brilliant future in which he could help save the lives of hundreds of thousands of people. We don't see Pax's long, hard, degrading experience as "bad" and "unfortunate." We see it as a blessing.

At Passages, we make available to our clients a white latex bracelet that has inscribed on it the words *"It's Perfect!"* It's a talisman of sorts. A talisman, by definition, is an object that holds supernatural properties and that provides a particular power, energy, and benefit to the possessor. The longer one wears a talisman or carries it, the more powerful the talisman becomes.

The bracelet is a reminder to those who wear it, many of whom have been through very tough times, that *if it happened, it's perfect, and I should treat it that way.* It's a reminder that situations are in our lives for one purpose only—so we can gain wisdom, information, understanding, and strength by working our way through them. When we have obtained the information we are meant to learn from those situations, they will pass out of our lives because we will have learned what was needed and changed accordingly—in this case, from being dependent on drugs and/or alcohol to being happily free of addiction.

In kindergarten or first grade, you learn that one plus one equals two. You don't get that lesson in college because you already know that; you don't need that lesson any longer. It's the same in all aspects of our lives. Once you have gotten all you need from a situation, it passes out of your life, never to return.

The next time you feel anger or fear about a situation, say to yourself: *There is information in this situation that I need, and I will get it by going through this. I will search for what I need to know about why this situation is in my life, keeping uppermost in my mind that this is a perfect contribution to the continuing stream of my life.*

Here's another incident that confirmed for me that every event that takes place is for our complete benefit. In 1993 I had one of my life's greatest experiences. Pax and I were out having an adventure in my old Chevy truck, gathering rocks for a landscape project for my son Todd. In a Malibu canyon off Pacific Coast Highway we saw a rock sticking up above the edge of a deep ravine. The eight inches of the rock we could see looked interesting and we stopped to take a closer look at it. The triangular-shaped rock was about twenty inches long and three-quarters buried in dirt except for the narrow portion I could see that projected above the roadside. I climbed down into the steep ravine until I was below the rock.

It was early morning and the dew was still on the ground making it slippery. I kicked my feet into the side of the slope to create a toehold in the dirt to stand on and cleared away the dirt around the rock that was holding it in place so I could get my hands underneath it to push it up onto the road. It weighed about a hundred and twenty pounds. I pushed and heaved until it was at the teeter-totter point where it was just about to fall over onto the road when my feet slipped out of the toehold and I slid thirty-five feet to the bottom of the ravine, my hands braced against the side of the ravine to hold myself upright.

What I didn't know was that the rock was hurtling down the ravine after me. It landed squarely on top of my head, driving me to the ground with such force that I had welts on my knees from the force with which I was slammed into the ground and two broken bones in my hand. It sounded to me as if a baseball bat had been broken on my head. My scalp had a huge gash and blood was seeping out. Amazingly, I didn't lose consciousness, but my vertebrae had compressed, pinching the nerves, and I was paralyzed from the neck down.

I was lying face down in the mud. I couldn't move and couldn't breathe. Can you imagine what I was I thinking?

My only thought was *I wonder what good thing will come of this?* Not for an instant did I lament any part of it—not the pain, not the paralysis, not the fact that I was lying in a shallow puddle of water and couldn't move or breathe. Not then, not now, and not for any instant in between did I think anything but *I wonder what good thing will come of this?*

Pax slid to the bottom of the ravine and rolled me over. He shouted, "Are you okay?" I was, but I couldn't move. As I lay there, my vertebrae began to decompress. Have you ever hit the funny bone in your elbow? That's what my whole body felt like as the decompression set in. It was the wildest sensation I have ever experienced.

Can you imagine the months, even years of lament I would have suffered if I did not know that that event was for my benefit? How I would have cursed my bad luck, how I would have suffered, thinking how unlucky I had been. How thoughts of "Why me? Why so bad? Why so hard?" would have ruined a good portion of my life.

Two weeks after my rock incident, as I was lying in bed, I discovered the gift that was meant to come to me from this incident. Although I had studied the English translations of the I Ching for decades, there were still many phrases I couldn't understand, as the book was written in Chinese three thousand years ago and that ancient language was and still is in the form of pictographs, word pictures. All of the English translations varied greatly. So as I was lying there in bed, I opened the I Ching. Most of the phrases that had baffled me for twenty years were suddenly crystal clear.

That smash on my head had opened channels that permitted me to understand much of what had perplexed me. Since then, I have written seven books on the I Ching, including my own version of the I Ching. The wisdom I have gained from that great book has been my guiding light. For a gift like that, I would get hit by a rock every year. Even to this day, as I read the I Ching for its eternal wisdom, I always bless the day that Tao gave me the gift of being smashed on my head by a rock so I would be able to better understand the great wisdom of the I Ching as well as how to use it to obtain Tao's information and guidance. More on the I Ching later.

We Determine the Outcome of Events

Lest you think those examples don't apply to your everyday life, here's one more story about how adapting to changing events and looking at them in a positive light can create a positive outcome. You may have experienced something like this yourself.

Years ago I had a brand-new car and I had parked it in the narrow alley next to my house. I walked out of the house just in time to see an old VW van scrape the front fender of the car as it moved through the narrow space between my car and the wall. The driver got out, threw his hat on the ground, then hung his head, holding it in his hands. He obviously had no money to pay for the damage to my car. His wife was in his car and his son was in the back seat crying. When the man saw me coming, he looked even more distraught. I walked up to the car, looked at him, and said: "Perfect. That's just what my car needed."

He couldn't believe what he was hearing.

"What did you say?" he blurted out.

I told him that I had been worried about parking my car in the alley and I didn't have to worry anymore because now the car was scratched. I said that it was a perfect event and that he and his family should have a nice day and not worry about the scrape.

He began crying tears of happiness and hugged me. He danced a little jig, ran around and got his family out of the car, and introduced them to me. He told me that he had just arrived in town, that he was a carpenter, and that they were looking for a place to stay until he could find work. Then the benefit of this event started to unfold.

I gave him the phone number of a friend of mine who was in the construction business, and the next day he began working for my friend. Three weeks later, this man showed up at my house to give me two hundred dollars to repair the scratch. I told him to keep it, that I liked the scratch because it reminded me of what a wonderful place our universe is.

To me, it was worth the damage to my car just to see how happy that man and his family were when I told him that his scratching my car was a perfect event. I still think about it to this day and it still makes me happy.

I never did repair the damage. When people would ask me how I scratched the car, I would say, "It's a gift from the universe." When they asked me to explain what I meant by that, I would tell them of my philosophy, and I was able to lead many people into a new way of understanding that stood them in good stead. On several occasions, the people I had spoken to told me that they had come to see seemingly bad events in their lives as a "scratch on the fender."

Suppose I had not reacted the way I had when my car had gotten scratched. Suppose I had instead punched the driver of the VW van and, after a violent fight, we had both wound up in jail. Suppose I had been sexually molested in jail, had gotten into another fight, had seriously hurt someone, and had been sentenced to twenty years in prison.

All of life presents us with two basic ways to treat events. We can either label them "good for us" or "bad for us."

Again, the event is only an event. It's how we treat an event that determines what it becomes in our lives. The event doesn't make that determination—we do.

Here is something that I wrote in my book *I Ching Wisdom Volume Two* that applies here: "To be joyous of heart is to hold an optimistic outlook, to see adversity as opportunity, to see failure as the starting point of success, to view our stubbed toes as the release of acupuncture points, to wake with a feeling of gratitude, and to sleep with a sustaining, unfaltering trust in Tao and in Tao's presence, of which we are a part. The person with a joyous heart is a treasure to be with, a wellspring of inspiration, and a fit companion. When we are joyous of heart, we hear a resonance in the songs of the birds, see resonance in the opening of a flower, and feel it in the pressure of a friend's hand. . . .

"Everything that happens, happens at the only possible time it can happen, and it is always at exactly the right time. We cannot get to an appointment before we arrive—or after. It is only at the instant of our arrival that we can arrive, and that is always at exactly the right moment, the perfect moment, the only possible moment." When you're arriving late for an important meeting, it's your attitude about your tardy arrival that will set the tone for the meeting.

It's also true that when you're angry or aggravated or just upset about something that has happened, even for an hour, that hour is lost. It has slipped by, unnoticed. The sun set, unnoticed. The waterfall you drove past fell a hundred feet, unnoticed. The lovely bird sang her heart out, unheard. The wonderful memory of your best friend went unremembered.

When you live by the philosophy that "unfolding events are perfect" and that "everything that happens benefits me," you are living an authentic life, a life at one with Tao, who brought about the events. Why? Because you are living in harmony with the way Tao manifests your destiny. As the Tao Te Ching tells us, Tao alone leads everything to fulfillment and perfection, making everything complete.

Let's explore a few more perspectives on life

that help us stay in harmony with Tao's intention for us, starting with how to take control of your life by taking control of your thoughts, how Tao figures into the picture, and what this means for you.

Your Mind, Your Brain, and Tao

When we talk about thoughts, first we have to understand the difference between our mind and our brain. Our brain is an intricate command center. There are about eighty-six billion neurons, or nerve cells, in our brain and about the same number of other cells. Our brain, three pounds consisting largely of fat and water in the upper third of our skull, is complex. Brain activity is made possible by the interconnections of neurons and their release of neurotransmitters in response to nerve impulses. Communication takes place through trillions of connections called synapses. A synapse is the minute space between two nerve cells where nerve impulses are relayed by a neurotransmitter.

We have more than a hundred different kinds of neurotransmitters. Six do most of the work:

acetylcholine, dopamine, norepinephrine, sero-tonin, GABA, and glutamate. Dopamine is the one that causes us to feel good by stimulating a small area of our brain, the nucleus accumbens, that is related to reward and reinforcement and the regulation of slow-wave sleep. It also plays its part in addiction.

Hippocrates, regarded as the Father of Medicine (approx. 460–370 BCE), said more than two thousand years ago: "Men ought to know that from nothing else but the brain come joys, delights, laughter, and sports, and sorrows, griefs, despondency, and lamentations. . . . All these things we endure from the brain."

Your brain is where everything is stored, including memories (a terrifying first day of school), information (2 + 2 = 4), events (the day you were hugely embarrassed as a child), and a complete record of everything you've ever learned, saw, thought, or experienced. Your brain stores all of it.

Your mind uses what's stored in your brain to extract information: What's Aunt Matilda's phone number? To carry out actions: "Raise right arm." To create movement: "Run!" You don't tell your brain to lift your right arm or to run; you just lift your arm or run. But it's your mind that's ordering your brain to do that.

Your mind evaluates: "It's a beautiful day." It wonders: "I wonder how many stars are in our universe?" It plans: "Next summer we're going to take a vacation to Yellowstone National Park." It creates: "This is my new sculpture." It philosophizes: "I believe that humans are sometimes well-intentioned and sometimes really nasty." Our mind is the "watcher" that seems to be outside of us, watching our every action and thought, analyzing everything.

Here are a few more examples of how your brain and mind work together so you can see how information stored in your brain can influence the decisions you make and actions you take: "The last time it rained I got soaked, so this time I'll take my umbrella." "I saw a movie about strange creatures that live in darkness and now I'm afraid to go out at night." "I was raped as a child and now I'm afraid to be physically close with anyone." "I was picked on when I was in school and now I believe people are basically mean."

Yes, your mind is influenced by the content

stored in your brain, but you can go beyond that input from the past as you consciously use your mind to tap in to Tao. When we use our mind, not our brain, to think, to imagine, to plan, to wonder about existence, we are drawing upon the Taoversal consciousness that streams through us.

Our consciousness is not separate from
Tao's consciousness. It is Tao's consciousness.
Tao's consciousness flows through us and
around us and is everywhere in everything.

What wondrousness that is. Within Tao's consciousness reside all wisdom, all ideas, and all information, including information that will be released to us when we are ready for it—today, tomorrow, or thousands of years from tomorrow.

As you learned at the beginning of this book, every new idea you've ever had, or anyone has ever had, was drawn from Tao's bank of information. Imagine the consciousness of Tao as a clear vapor, perfectly clear, invisible to us. An aware vapor without physical substance—only consciousness, awareness—containing *all knowledge and all information*. Existing everywhere in everything. Permeating every fiber of us, activating us, providing us with information and knowledge when we need it or when we are ready for it. That's what consciousness is like, what consciousness *is*.

Controlling Your Mind

What's stored in your brain can seriously damage you, but kept under the control of your mind, nothing can help you as much. Say your brain is loaded with harmful information (that is in all of us). It could be worries about your life condition, illness, debts, lack of money and the problems that could bring, a failing marriage, failing business, failing health, problems with family, lack of friends, being in pain, wrongs done to you by others, including the courts, legal affairs, enemies, feelings of inadequacy, wrongs you have done to others, feelings of resentment, revenge, hatred—any kind of difficulty in your life.

As a result of that information, your brain can feed your mind powerful stress. When your mind is occupied with unpleasant, stressful, even scary thoughts, produced by what's stored in your brain, it can cause you unhappiness, poor health, turmoil, unrest, concern, anxiety, sleeplessness, visions of problems, visions of hopelessness, and physical sensations that can spoil or ruin the quality of your life.

Those are what Shakespeare called "a sea of troubles," so burdensome that Hamlet, one of Shakespeare's characters, was considering suicide. But Shakespeare, speaking through Hamlet, also knew that by opposing his "sea of troubles," he could end them. As Shakespeare wrote: "To be, or not to be, that is the question: Whether 'tis nobler in the mind to suffer the slings and arrows of outrageous fortune, *or to take arms against a sea of troubles and by opposing, end them."*

How is that done? By the reasoning power of your mind. By controlling what your mind focuses its attention on.

Taking control of your life begins with taking control of your thoughts.

You can take what you have learned from the knowings in this book and safely and powerfully put an end to your suffering. All the information is here for you.

Take control of your life by taking control

of your mental condition and by putting your new philosophy to work. Talk to Tao, not with pleading or begging but as if you're talking to a good friend.

Tao chose you. Now you choose Tao.

Your brain, left unattended, will focus on what is of concern in your life. That's perfect because that's how you find solutions to your problems. It's only when you let it get out of control and you begin to let the information in your brain infect your mind with misgivings, concerns, and wild imaginings that it will cause you more damage and unhappiness than almost anyone can bear.

Do not allow your brain to infect your mind with visions of ill health, problems, unhappiness, and conflict. *You* are in charge. Do not succumb to loading your brain with garbage. Stop living in the "Garbage Inn." It is loaded with the junk of your life. *Clear it out.*

Can you do it? Of course you can.

Put your brain in order by supplying it with new information. Saturate it with good thoughts, happy thoughts, with visons of a perfect future, a happy future.

As we talked about, you can also free yourself

of burdens from the past by seeing the seemingly bad events as part of the chain of circumstances that led you to the pleasurable or fortunate events or circumstances you later experienced or that exist in your life today. The pleasurable events were a direct result of the seemingly bad events. Here's an example.

In 2007, I was giving interviews for my book *The Alcoholism and Addiction Cure.* When one reporter came to the interview, I could smell the powerful aroma of alcohol on his breath. It was so strong I commented on it. He said, "Yes, I drink quite a bit every day." I asked him why he did that and he said it was because he was the victim of a missed opportunity early on in his life. I asked him to tell me about it.

The reporter said that when he was twenty-one he had an opportunity to go to a prestigious university, but he chose not to go. He said he occasionally got an interview assignment from his sister, who was an editor at the newspaper, and that his real job was driving a truck delivering bread, milk, and eggs at three o'clock in the morning. He blamed his early decision not to attend the prestigious university when he was in his twenties for his current unhappy job situation. I asked him if he was married and he told me that he was married and had six children. I asked if he loved his wife and children. He said they were the joy of his life, the best thing that had ever happened to him.

I asked him if he had gone to another college, and he said he had, but it was a small, little-known college. I asked if anything unusual or special had happened at that college and he said, "Yes, that's where I met my wife."

I was amazed. "And you're unhappy that you didn't go to the other university?" I said. "You must be a madman! That's the best thing that ever happened to you!"

I saw that all his years of disappointment and drinking had been over an event that was, in reality, a huge benefit to him. After he thought about it a minute, he said, "You know, you're right." A few months later, I received a letter from his sister thanking me, telling me that her brother had quit drinking and was a changed man. That is how empowering it can be to change what you think about events, past or present.

When your mind takes over, which it can, and

feeds your brain new information and direction, and constantly reaffirms that new information, you benefit greatly. Take some time to review disturbing events, current or past, to see if you can find a view of them that fits into a perfect "now."

Call upon Tao to nurture and protect you. And do your part. Take what you have learned here about life, about Tao, and about you and Tao to create a happy place in which you will reside in peace, safety, and comfort.

You can do this! Is it hard? *Absolutely.* We've been slaves to what's stored in our brain for so long that it takes a herculean effort to clear it out. But it is essential for a good life that you do.

Before we move on, let's look at two more keys to living an authentic life that can immediately help you on your daily path toward enlightenment.

The Laws of Love

Certainly, in creating laws, Tao would not leave out the very important aspect of love. Actually, love may be the most important aspect of creation. To love deeply and completely, to love and be loved, is an exquisite gift. There is probably no emotion that can benefit us more.

Just as there are laws that regulate everything in the Taoverse, there are laws that regulate every aspect of our lives, especially love. *The Laws of Love,* a book I wrote in 2012, sets forth the universal laws that regulate love and makes the point that having the relationship of your dreams does not depend on luck; it depends first on Tao providing you with a partner and then on you working with your partner using the guidance of the laws of love. I will share one of the most significant guidelines for creating the relationship of your dreams. I learned it from my friend Carl Hartman in Big Sur, California. He called it "Safe Space."

Draw an imaginary circle around you and your partner. It's the circle of Safe Space. Within that circle, your partner cannot do *anything* you will find fault with: crash the car, forget to make the plane reservations, forget to bring home the grocery item you requested, burn the dinner, lose your briefcase with your timely work in it, lose the keys to your home or car, break your most treasured possession, or any of thousands of examples like those or worse. Harsh criticism, anger, sarcasm, yelling, and intolerance of any kind are not permitted in the circle of Safe Space. Lying about anything is not permitted—not even tiny or seemingly insignificant distortions of the truth. All the truth, all the time.

Absolute trust must exist. That's the space where trust is born and true love develops.

Wouldn't you like to live in such a space?

How large is the circle? It encompasses your entire lives, together or apart. Within that circle, trust is born, love grows, and life and love flourish. Without trust and without Safe Space, your relationship will never achieve its sublime potential and you will live forever in a less-than-fulfilling, less-than-rewarding relationship that will be of your own creation—a second-class relationship.

When I finished writing *The Laws of Love*, Lyn asked if she could write something in the new book. Here's what she wrote: "I have now lived with my husband, Chris, for eleven years and they have been the happiest years of my life." Sharing a relationship with someone who feels that way about you is a sublime experience. Create that.

Enjoying the Moment

Another principle that will help you immeasurably as you learn to live in harmony with Tao is a concept you might not associate with the path of enlightened living. Nevertheless, it will help you apply what you are learning here and help you to become more in tune with Tao.

My book *Be Who You Want, Have What You Want* has fourteen chapters, and at the end of most of the chapters I included a few exercises. Reading the book without doing the exercises will give you intellectual information, but we need more than that. We need to learn how to put the concepts to work in our life. Fulfilling the exercises is where the magic happens. Every exercise in a chapter must be completed before going on to the next chapter.

One of the exercises, "Enjoy a half hour of pleasure," is an exercise that is repeated in many of the chapters. Most of us do not know how to create pleasure or how to stay in the present moment to enjoy it. In completing the pleasure exercises in the book, one has to fully enjoy a half hour of pleasure. If something mars the reader's half hour of pleasure, the reader must start over at the time of their choosing, not reading further until the exercise is completed.

For instance, if you chose to walk on a favorite path for half an hour, and on your walk something happens to distract you from experiencing pleasure, I ask you to gently bring your awareness back to your goal—which is to enjoy a full half hour of pleasure—and then begin another half hour exercise, then or later.

That is a wonderful, life-giving, life-saving exercise. It's part of what I talked about earlier: *To slow down time and add years to your life, practice enjoying the moment. It's where you spend your entire life.*

Enjoying the moment is a powerful way to get in touch with the delights of Tao that infuse our world and our life. Those delights go by unnoticed when we are so easily overshadowed by distractions, worries, and the tyranny of negative thoughts.

When you engage in a half hour of pleasure, you purposely direct your thoughts away from anything that detracts from your pleasurable state of mind. You have twenty-three and a half hours left in the day to worry or to let negative thoughts plague you. With the "Enjoy a half hour of pleasure" exercise, you are training your mind to find pleasure and also to protect itself from the invasion of unpleasant thoughts.

This exercise is not something you should "try." *Try,* when used in the past tense, *tried,* means you failed—such as "I tried to climb the mountain, but it snowed and I had to quit" or "I tried to pass the exam, but it was too hard for me." So this is not something you should *try.* It's something you should *do*—regularly.

Take half an hour and enjoy yourself. You deserve it. Make it a ritual, perhaps once a week, and the benefits will soon become apparent. Learning how to fully enjoy yourself is an art, and you can most certainly learn that art.

Accessing Tao's
Guidance

*"Because we are one with Tao,
we can know everything Tao knows and
receive guidance when we need it."*

6
....

Accessing Tao's Guidance

If you knew which of your actions would bring you good fortune and which misfortune, which actions would lead to your success and which to failure, wouldn't that knowledge be better than gold and diamonds? Wouldn't it allow you to achieve any goal? Provide you with the best chance to avoid the inevitable pitfalls that beset the path of every endeavor, project, or venture? If you could transcend the barriers of time to look into the future, into the past, if you could see the road that led to happiness and the road that led to despair, wouldn't you consider yourself fortunate indeed?

Earlier we explored the idea that you and Tao are in a partnership, even though you may not always be aware of it, and that because you are a part of the Taoverse, you can be in two-way communication with Tao. There are many ways of gaining access to the information and guidance Tao makes available.

Vast numbers of divination methods have been used over thousands of years, actually throughout the entire history of humans, to access Tao's guidance—heating tortoise shells until they cracked and then reading the cracks, oracles such as the Delphic oracle in ancient Greece who could predict the future or answer questions, tarot cards, oil gazing, water gazing, mirror gazing, Ouija boards, reading tea leaves in the bottom of a cup after drinking the tea, dreams, horoscopes (reading the positions of the planets and stars), even flipping a coin, and hundreds, maybe thousands of other methods. As you read in chapter 4, I was fortunate to meet an oracle who made a profound difference in my life.

The reason these ways to receive guidance work is that we are part of the Taoverse and the methods are part of the Taoverse. We can extract information from the Taoverse because everything comes from, is made from the same source: Tao. And to assist us, Tao has provided us the means to obtain Taoversal information.

In other words, because we are one with Tao, we can know everything Tao knows and receive guidance when we need it. All we need is a key to unlock that fount of sublime wisdom and complete information. The method of receiving guidance that has always worked best for me is the I Ching (pronounced "yee djing" in Chinese), one of the oldest books in the world.

An Ancient Guide to Universal Wisdom

I discovered the I Ching in 1972. I was in London negotiating with Rank Film Distributors for the distribution of my movie *Goin' Home,* which I was still working on. I stopped to browse in a used bookstore and came across the Princeton University Press edition of the I Ching translated by Richard Wilhelm and Carey F. Baynes. I didn't know what the book was, but I opened it and read at random in a few places. I saw that it contained universal laws. The entire book, over seven hundred pages, was devoted almost entirely to informing a reader what an enlightened person would do in every situation to achieve success and avoid failure and to act as a "superior person" would act—that is, honorably.

The creation of the I Ching is attributed to Fu Hsi ("foo shee"), a Chinese sage known only in legend, as he lived five thousand years ago, a thousand or more years before writing or numbers developed in China. Fu Hsi's wisdom had been passed along in the oral tradition, one generation teaching another, as a long poem for easy memorization. Approximately thirty-five hundred years ago, when writing began in China, Fu Shi's wisdom was the basis for the first book written in that language, the I Ching.

The wisdom of the I Ching played a major role in the development of the Chinese civilization. With it, the people learned how to build houses, use a ridgepole to support roofs, and use the plow, the hoe, the shovel, gunpowder, and many kinds of devices. They also used it as a guide for overseeing the country, for warfare, and for obtaining guidance for every important action and decision, including marriage, relationships, statesmanship, contracts, and life in general. That persisted until roughly two hundred and fifty years ago, when a new regime came into power that wanted to do away with the ability of the people to receive guidance from Tao. However, there are still a few communities in China whose residents live according to I Ching precepts and guidance.

In those early days when the knowledge and application of the I Ching flourished, to obtain employment in a government position one had to take a test in the use of the I Ching. The book was also used as an oracle, a way of foretelling the future. I define *oracle* as a person or object, such as a book of answers, from which advice, prophecies, or spiritual guidance can be obtained.

The I Ching was spared in the great book burning that took place in China in 213 BCE under the reign of Ch'in (or Yin) Shih Huang Ti, who wanted to stamp out opposing political views and thought. No doubt those in power thought that by keeping the people simple and uneducated, the people would be happy and content and not think about overthrowing the elite. Fortunately, the I Ching was protected because the rulers needed to be able to peer into the future and make decisions regarding the ruling of the dynasty and the outcome of their plans.

The I Ching as an Oracle

When I first learned about the I Ching, I spent hours every day studying it to see what the ancient Chinese masters knew of the universe, human nature, and the ways of the world. Understanding the I Ching was a substantial problem for me from the beginning. Many of the phrases in the book were beyond me, such as "flying dragon mounts to the sky," "a yellow garment brings good fortune," "the taming power of the small has success," "ten pairs of tortoises cannot oppose it," "a crane calling in the shade; its young answers it." I didn't know what those phrases meant. I studied the I Ching for three years before I began using it as an oracle, a way of communicating with the universe.

When I was again in England, to raise money to make my film, I put an ad in *The Times* for an assistant. Five men answered the ad. I interviewed them together in my hotel room, which had a separate living room. They were all qualified and I didn't know which one to choose. I excused myself and went into my bedroom and picked up the I Ching and talked to Tao.

"I don't know how to use this book as an oracle," I said, "but I know that there is some part of me that knows everything in this book. I'm going to open it and I need to know which of these men to choose as my assistant."

I opened to the page with the six-line figure (known as a hexagram) numbered 45, Gathering Together, and the explanation there said: "In the time of gathering together, we should make no arbitrary choices. There are secret forces at work leading together those who belong together."

Since that didn't give me specific guidance but said not to make an arbitrary choice, I went back to the men and told them I couldn't decide that day but would be in touch with them. By the end of the week, four of the men were not responding to my communication. The fifth came back to my hotel and said, "This is my job. I'll be your best assistant ever." He was. That's when I realized that we are able to communicate with our spiritual source using the I Ching.

Now almost fifty years have passed since I discovered the I Ching, and I still read it regularly and use it as a guide. The wisdom of the I Ching is inexhaustible. As for the ability to obtain guidance from Tao, well, I don't know how anyone can get along without it.

Ancient Chinese writing was, as I've said, in the form of pictographs, or word pictures. All the translations of the I Ching are therefore slightly different, as each translator interprets the pictographs differently. Since there was much in the book I couldn't understand at first, I longed for a deeper understanding, as it was becoming the mainstay of my life, my lodestar.

In general usage, a lodestar is a star that is used to guide the course of a ship, especially Polaris, the North Star. I use *lodestar* to mean a spiritual source of wisdom, information, and guidance that leads us unerringly on a path that is just, good, right, honorable, in our best interest, and in the best interest of everyone.

> *Every person must have something to follow—*
> *a guiding light, a lodestar—if they are to move*
> *safely and successfully through the affairs of*
> *the world.*

Having a lodestar helps us avoid the pitfalls that beset all our paths. The knowings are such lodestars.

After years of studying and working with the I Ching, in 1995 I wrote my own version of the I Ching, entitled *The I Ching: The Book of Answers,* to make it easier to ask and get the answers to questions. Years later, I published a revised edition. I wrote that book under my Chinese pen name, Wu Wei. I didn't want anything to stand in the way of the reader and the wisdom, such as me being a Caucasian, so I chose the name Wu Wei, which means, in essence, taking no unnatural action or not taking any action that is not in accord with the natural course of the Taoverse. Now my son Pax, a master of the I Ching, is finishing his version, which by far exceeds all the other versions, including mine. Pax has been using the I Ching for nearly thirty years and has performed thousands of readings in his business life, creating Passages with me, and in his personal life since he was eighteen.

Moving through the Stages of Change

To access guidance from Tao, a reference book is required to provide answers that will guide you to achieve success and avoid failure in every situation along with a method to choose the correct answer. The teachings of Fu Hsi and the I Ching provide just that, a way of communicating with Tao.

In Chinese, *I* means "change" and *Ching* means "book"—"The Book of Changes." It is so called because everything is in a constant state of change, and the lines of the hexagrams in the I Ching reflect that constant motion. Through a specific method of dividing forty-nine yarrow stalks (stems of the milfoil plant), we can receive answers to our questions, obtain direction, anticipate changes, avoid dangers, and take the correct action to bring about the most beneficial results.

I've talked about change throughout this book. All situations, including the ones you are going through now, proceed through six stages of change: about to come into being, beginning, expanding, approaching maximum potential, peaking, and finally passing their peak and flowing into their new condition. *Everything in existence is flowing through the six stages of change.*

Change is like a stream. Everything is different every instant, continually moving through the stages of change. We, too, in our lives, in our understanding, in our spiritual growth, and in our physical life are following those six stages of change. Sometimes you may go back and forth between one stage or another. Sometimes you may stay in one stage longer than another. But in the end the six stages always manifest.

Since everything in life is moving through the stages of change, learning to understand and welcome change is essential.

As Alan Watts (1915-1973), renowned interpreter of Asian philosophies, said: "The only way to make sense out of change is to plunge into it, move with it, and join the dance."

The ancient Chinese sages referred to Tao as the "The Creative," and in one commentary on the I Ching, attributed to Confucius, that great sage explains: "The way of the Creative [Tao] is to change and alter each of us until we all achieve our true nature, and then to keep us living in accord with the Great Harmony." The I Ching, then, helps us understand, adapt to, and work with change. When giving us guidance, it makes us aware of how a situation changes as it progresses and provides guidance to help us adapt to and make the most of the changes.

Not only our lives but all civilizations go through the six stages of change. By looking into the history of civilizations, we can see the current or past stages of development and decline. Leaders have a great deal to do with the rise and fall of civilizations. Only leaders who seek to benefit the whole of the people rise to greatness and bring their countries to greatness. They are the ones who are revered by the people they rule.

All separatist tendencies work against the benefit of the people. From the Bible: "Every kingdom divided against itself is brought to desolation; and every city or house divided against itself shall not stand" and "Those who trouble their own house will inherit the wind." Those sayings are also true for relationships. In my book *The Laws of Love,* I go into greater detail about those changes and how your relationship is affected by them.

A Working Model of the Taoverse

In the time of Fu Hsi, we humans needed a boost, a way to accelerate our progress to enlightenment and understanding. Tao chose Fu Hsi to receive a great knowing. He was given the symbols of the life force of the Taoverse and an understanding that enabled him to interpret the symbols to gain information. Fu Hsi was aware that he was part of an alive, conscious Taoverse and that as such he could communicate with it. Tao provided him with an oracle, a way to receive guidance from Tao.

According to writings of great antiquity, there are two versions of the way the information that is the basis for the I Ching was revealed to Fu Hsi. One is that a large tortoise emerged from China's Li River to show itself to Fu Hsi. On the back of its shell were the eight three-line symbols, known as the "bagua" or the eight trigrams. Another story says that a wild horse appeared that had the symbols on its side. When Tao wants to communicate with us, Tao uses whatever means are at hand. (My small book *A Tale of the I Ching* tells the story of how I believe the I Ching began. It will open the heart of that great book for you.)

As you can see on the facing page, each of the eight trigrams (bagua) is composed of three lines, either broken or unbroken, placed one above the other. In approximately the twelfth century BCE, King Wen, ruler of a province in northwest China, discovered that by combining each trigram with itself and with each of the other trigrams, sixty-four figures are created (8 x 8 = 64). Those sixty-four lined figures are each made up of six lines (for a total of 384 lines). The meanings of each of the 384 lines were interpreted by King Wen's son, the Duke of Chou, otherwise known as Dan, during the time he was acting ruler. English-speaking people call the six-line figures hexagrams. The Chinese call them kua (or gua).

Each of the trigrams and hexagrams has a Chinese name that expresses its meaning. The meaning of each kua is generally derived from the attributes of the two trigrams from which it is

The Eight Bagua

☰

CH'IEN

THE CREATIVE

☷

K'UN

THE RECEPTIVE

☳

CHÊN

AROUSING

☴

SUN

WIND, WOOD

☵

K'AN

WATER, THE ABYSS

☲

LI

FIRE

☶

KÊN

MOUNTAIN

☱

T'UI

MARSH, LAKE

T'ai

The Sixty-Four Kua

https://commons.wikimedia.org/wiki/
File:King_Wen_(I_Ching).svg

formed. For example, one of the kua is called T'ai, which stands for "heaven on earth" or "peace." The top trigram represents earth, the lower trigram heaven. The tendency of earth is to sink and the tendency of heaven is to rise. The two come together to produce the condition of "peaceful prosperity, harmony, heaven on earth."

The text of the I Ching describing this kua, as I interpret it in my version of the I Ching, reads: "What a wonderful time of perfect harmony this is! The light force is in the ascendency, and the dark force is diminishing. People in high places are considerate of their subordinates, subordinates are helpful and respectful to those in power, feuds end, friendships are renewed, peace prevails, and pettiness ends. People act from their higher natures rather than from their lower. There is perfect correspondence in all areas, meaning that everyone is at peace with everyone else. This is a time of good fortune and success, when even your small efforts will bring great rewards. This time can be lengthened if conflicts are resolved and you make an extra effort to get along with others by being as courteous and considerate as you can. In this way, all can share in the blessings of this time.

"Savor what it feels like when everything goes right, when conflict disappears, when your plans are easily fulfilled, and your goals are obtained almost effortlessly. In such a time of peaceful harmony, it is easy to end long-standing arguments, resolve difficult situations, and bring about peace. Be reverent and grateful for this magical time of peace and do all you can to make it last as long as possible."

The I Ching's sixty-four six-line symbols are, in essence, *a working model of our Taoverse*. Each of the sixty-four kua (with their six lines each) represents an evolving condition or situation, and the I Ching gives the meaning related to each line. When you use the yarrow stalks for identifying one of the sixty-four kua in answer to a question you have (I advise using only the yarrow-stalk method), the I Ching provides the exact guidance that is meant for you, revealing what action you should take to obtain the best outcome.

In short, the I Ching is a book of answers, and those answers are in the form of the sixty-four situations or conditions that the hexagrams represent. Furthermore, each situation or condition contains within it six stages of evolution, represented by the six lines of each hexagram. The entire book is also a guide to what an enlightened person does in every situation and a quintessential source of wisdom about how to live life as an ambassador of Tao. It is the best role model that exists. I have listed some of the characteristics of an enlightened person after the last chapter of this book.

Working with the I Ching to Obtain Guidance

DNA, short for deoxyribonucleic acid, was discovered in 1869. As defined at ScienceDaily, DNA is "a nucleic acid that contains the genetic instructions for the development and function of all living things. All known cellular life and some viruses contain DNA. The main role of DNA in the cell is the long-term storage of information."[1] DNA determines the color of your hair and eyes and literally everything else about your brain and body.

In 1953, the mathematical structure of the three-dimensional double helix of our DNA was discovered. By exchanging the I Ching's broken lines for zeros and the unbroken lines for ones, the result is the exact order of the mathematical structure of the double helix of DNA. It is also the exact order of the binary system, a system for writing any number using zeros and ones that is the basis for all computer language. Fu Hsi created that system before there was writing and before there were numbers. That was the great knowing given to Fu Hsi.

As if that wasn't enough, the system that was revealed to Fu Hsi and that has come down to us intact over thousands of years enabled him, and now enables us, to be able to communicate with the consciousness of our Taoverse—with Tao. By writing your questions and using the yarrow stalks to direct you to the particular answer in the I Ching that applies to your situation, you will be able to take advantage of life's opportunities and see your way through the seeming tragedies that occur in the lives of us all.

Once you have learned how to work with the I Ching, there will be no need to hopelessly wonder whether or not you should consider a relationship with someone, start a particular business, move to a particular neighborhood, go to a particular place on vacation, or take a particular action. You will get the answers to those questions and any of the thousands of other questions you face during your lifetime.

Here's just one short example out of hundreds where I received unerring guidance from the I Ching in answer to a question. I had planned a trip to Grand Cayman to visit a friend. My plan was to leave in three days. I did a reading: "What can I expect from a visit to the Cayman Islands in three days?" My answer was hexagram number 5, Waiting in the Face of Danger. The first few lines of the guidance said: "You are a strong person who desires to advance, but grave danger threatens your advance. The correct action is to wait until the danger passes, for to advance in the face of such danger would be foolhardy." I put off my trip. Four days later there was an uprising on the island and many people were injured. I waited until the uprising had subsided and did another reading. That reading indicated my trip would be crowned with sublime success, which it was.

When working with the I Ching, be aware, though, that you must do your part. When you get an answer to an I Ching reading that foretells success, for instance, it does not mean that success is inevitably forthcoming. Your actions from the time of reading the answer until the result is achieved will determine the success or failure of your efforts. Your well-intentioned efforts are always part of the equation.

Suppose you were thinking of running for public office and did a reading to determine what the outcome of the election would be. Let's say that you asked the question "What can I expect as a result of running for the office of mayor of my town?" Let's say that the answer you received was kua 19, Lin (Advancing, Progress), and the reading pointed you to this specific answer: "This is a fortunate time when your advances will be crowned with supreme success. You must make the best use of this time of rapid, easy advance by acting with great determination and perseverance, for it will not last forever. . . . During this time of rapid advance, be tireless in bringing your plans to completion. This is the time for action."

According to your reading, the result of your efforts will be "crowned with supreme success." However, if you take that to mean that no matter what you do you will be supremely successful, you may miss the mark completely and lose the election by a wide margin. You are instructed to "make the best use of this time of rapid, easy advance." If, instead of acting swiftly and entering the race for mayor, you take an extended vacation, you will most likely experience a dismal failure rather than a supreme success.

The I Ching is an oracle of inestimable value as long as you seek the truth with reverence and sincerity. The rest is up to you.

You can work with the I Ching to ask questions and get direction regarding any issue or concern—health, relationships, financial matters, social situations, business decisions, trips, undertakings of any kind, philosophical questions, and questions about people, events, or conditions. The I Ching can also alert you to unknown problems that may exist or situations that may begin to disintegrate. If you catch those problems at their beginnings, you can take preventive action. Left unattended, conditions can grow to such proportions that no action you take will prevent failure. It's a great comfort to know that no matter how monumental a problem, we can receive guidance in finding a solution to it.

You will also find it remarkably rewarding to set aside some time on your birthdays to ask, "What can I expect this birthday year?" Or "What do I have to pay attention to in order to have the most productive birthday year?" Similarly, on the first day of the new year, you can ask, "What does the new year hold in store for me?" Or "What can I do to have the most productive new year?"

If you decide to use the I Ching to enrich your life, I strongly recommend that you use yarrow stalks for the divination process—not coins, cards, or any other method. Three coins have only three heads and three tails and therefore do not possess sufficient variation to display the unfolding Taoverse. You will get an answer, but it may not be a complete or correct answer. The original method of using yarrow stalks works perfectly.

My interpretation of the I Ching in my book *The I Ching: The Book of Answers* is easy to use for purposes of divination while still being true to the ancient wisdom. I've also written several other books to help support you in learning how to work with the I Ching and access its guidance (see the list at the back of this book). It's easy. These books include details of exactly how to use yarrow stalks to arrive at the appropriate answer, how to ask questions, and how to interpret the guidance you receive as well as real-life examples of situations where people have consulted the I Ching and how it helped them. I've also created a workbook to make it easier for you to use the I Ching and to preserve your questions and answers.

It may seem self-serving for me to write about my books and to suggest that you purchase them, but I risk offending you and the critics to fulfill one of my goals for you—to obtain guidance from your Taoverse. I want you to live a better, richer, easier, more productive life. Over the ages, philosophers, warriors, statesmen, emperors, and people like you have consulted this ancient classic to seek direction in order to obtain good fortune. May this invaluable gift of wisdom and guidance now be a light for you while you are living your way to enlightenment, one with Tao.

You Are the Miracle

We have now completed what we began under this canopy of trees. I congratulate you. *I bow low to you, great spiritual traveler.* I cherish our magical time together. Having come so far, you have ascended into the realms where few venture. Those who exist at this level welcome you!

There is much to contemplate in what I have shared with you. I hope you will return here again and again for inspiration and to remind yourself of the truths about the Taoverse and about yourself that are of ultimate importance.

> *Remember: Enlightenment is knowing*
> *Who You Are in relation to All-That-Is.*

> *There is nothing in the Taoverse more the*
> *Taoverse than you. You always were; you*
> *will always be. You were chosen to be here*
> *then and now. And that is the miracle.*

> *We can conceive of "the One," the One*
> *I call Tao. And that is truly the miracle.*

> *And finally you—you are the miracle.*

In each of our lives, the curtain has gone up. We are each playing our part. And the curtain will soon go down. The play will have run. The story of our lives will be known. With whatever time is left to you, play your part well—perfectly. Play it as you want to be remembered. No more can anyone ask of us or can we ask of ourselves.

Tao's favorite tool for benefiting and
improving you is adversity. Welcome it.
Greet the future as a champion.

Wherever you go or whatever you do, no matter how hard or trying, keep living in mind and you will find that you'll always be living, not dying. In the light of the setting sun we either beat the pot and sing or loudly bewail the approach of old age.

I wish you well on your endless journey. In reflecting on what you have found here and acting in accord with what is highest and best within you, you can change your destiny. You will now discover what you seek. You will succeed greatly. You will prosper in all areas of life. You will find peace. You will find love.

The torch of enlightenment is now in your hands. Carry it proudly. Carry it with reverence. Carry it as a philosopher. Carry it as an ambassador of Tao.

Keep in mind, on planet Earth *everyone* has been chosen. Few know that.

Let your light shine brightly, as none need it so much as your fellow travelers whose light is dim.

I'm proud of you!

And so, we end our talk as we began it, sitting here under the trees. I have enjoyed our time together. Till we meet again, I wish you good fortune.

Your fellow traveler,

Chris

A Few Qualities of
the Enlightened Ones

"The ancient sages tell us that it is only through daily self-renewal of character that we can attain and continue at the height of our powers."

A Few Qualities of the Enlightened Ones

As I touched on in chapter 6, we all need a lodestar to follow—something to bring out the best in us and to provide direction for our development. The qualities of the enlightened ones are just such a source of wisdom and guiding light. By holding the image of the enlightened person in your mind as your lodestar, you will achieve not only supreme success but also great happiness as you live your way to enlightenment.

It takes herculean effort to reach the peak of perfection in any area of life and continuous effort to remain there. The ancient sages tell us that it is only through daily self-renewal of character that we can attain and continue at the height of our powers.

That is why it is wise to make some effort every day to refresh yourself in the ways of the enlightened person. Reading the great books, talking to like-minded people, studying the deeds of our ancient heroes, reading the words of our early philosophers, teaching others, thinking about your actions of the day to see whether you are being the best you can be—those are all ways to successfully continue on the path. As you grow in awareness, your power grows and your attainments will be like the harvest after a perfect summer. There is no other activity that rewards you as richly as the daily self-renewing of your character.

Here are some of the qualities of the enlightened ones.

They are humble.
They are willing to let others go ahead of them.
They are courteous.
Their good manners stem from their humility
    and concern for others.
They are good-natured.
They are calm.
They are always inwardly acknowledging the
    wonder they feel for all of creation.

They are willing to give others the credit.

They speak well of everyone, ill of no one.

They believe in themselves and in others.

They do not swear or use vulgarity.

They are physically fit.

They do not overindulge.

They know what is enough.

They can cheerfully do without.

They are willing to look within themselves
     to find the error.

They are true to what they believe.

They are gentle.

They are able to make decisions and act on them.

They are reverent.

They carry on their teaching activity.

They do not criticize or find fault unnecessarily.

They are willing to take blame.

They do not have to prove anything.

They are content within themselves.

They are dependable.

They are aware of danger.

They are certain of their right to be here.

They are certain of your right to be here.

They are aware of Tao's plan unfolding as
     it should.

They are generally happy.

They laugh easily.

They can cry.

It is all right with them if another wins.

Their happiness for another's happiness is sincere.

Their sorrow for another's sorrow is sincere.

They have no hidden agendas.

They are thrifty and therefore are not in want.

They find a use for everything.

They honor others and are therefore honored.

They pay attention to detail.

They are conscientious.

They value others and are therefore valued.

They are optimistic.

They are trustworthy.

They are good at salvage.

They are patient.

They know the value of silence.

They are peaceful.

They are generous.

They are considerate.

They are courageous in the face of fear.

They are clean.

They are tidy.

They do not shirk their duties.

They cause others to feel special.

They expect things to turn out well.

They seek to benefit others.

Their presence has a calming effect.

They are not attached to things.

They see obstruction as opportunity.

They see opposition as a signpost pointing them
in the right direction.

They set a good example.

They are joyous of heart.

They take thought for the future.

They waste nothing and therefore always
have enough.

They have good manners.

They have greatness of spirit.

They are clearheaded.

They do more than their share.

They meet others more than halfway.

They rest when it is time to rest; they act when
it is time to act.

They feel no bitterness.

They are forgiving.

They do not unnecessarily pretend.

They are not cynical.

They study.

They revere the ancient masters.

They are inspiring.

They nourish nature and are therefore nourished
by nature.

They leave things better than they found them.

They do not make a show.

They practice goodness.

They are simple.

Their intentions are always beneficial.

They are a wellspring of determination.

They do not boast.

They produce long-lasting effects.

They cultivate endurance.

They are flexible in their thinking.

They do not overreach themselves.

They do not overspend themselves.

They do not strive foolishly.

They are consistent.

They do not go into unnecessary debt.

They live a simple life.

They nurture their good qualities and virtues.

They are sensitive to their inner promptings.

They exist in the present.

They feel no break with time. Knowing they had
past lives, knowing they will have future lives,
their lives, including their current life, are like
the ebb and flow of the oceans.

They are cautious.

They are kind.

They hold their goals lightly in mind, allow no
opposing thoughts to enter, and, as a result of
natural law, are drawn to their goals.

They seek enlightenment.

They set limitations for themselves within which
they experience complete freedom.

They are careful of their words, knowing they
are reflected in them.

They do not use flattery.

They depend on themselves for happiness.

They feel secure.

They know the truth of their existence.

They do not complain.

They turn back immediately whenever they
discover that they have strayed from the path
of the enlightened person.

They practice daily self-renewal of their
character.

Consciousness Drained of Doubt

by Dermot OBrien

I waited
On this idyllic island
Sun Drenched
Ocean Swept
I waited
All these years
But still I sought Thee
Then I caught a glimpse
On the Dragonfly's latticed wings
And from a glimmer on the iridescent clouds
That rolled in from the Bahamas
Straight up
Intense
Remember when We saw it in Bethesda
The Potomac
Flowing
Pulsating
Everywhere
Our Consciousness Drained of Doubt
Aware of It
It aware of Us
Samadhi

Or in the Temple at Borobudur
When all the religions were One
These fragments
Being made Whole
Six lines
Always changing
One on top of the other
Forever
Like a gigantic clock
Satori
As death approaches
It brings me closer
Is that fear
of the unknown
Or a window opening
Beckoning
me
to
Belong
to
Each
Moment
Present
Now

Copyright © Dermot Obrien

Endnotes

Chapter 2

1. Witter Bynner, *The Way of Life, According to Lao Tzu* (New York: Perigree, 1986), 33.

Chapter 3

1. Walter Isaacson, *Einstein: His Life and Universe* (New York: Simon & Schuster, 2007), 549.

2. For information on the first images capturing a black hole, see: https://www.nature.com/articles/d41586-019-01155-0 (accessed February 14, 2021); https://www.space.com/first-black-hole-image-polarized-m87 (accessed July 23, 2021); https://eventhorizontelescope.org/blog/astronomers-image-magnetic-fields-edge-m87s-black-hole (accessed July 23, 2021).

3. Wikipedia contributors, "Singularity," *Wikipedia, The Free Encyclopedia*, https://en.wikipedia.org/w/index.php?title=Singularity&oldid=1064002245 (accessed April 1, 2022).

4. Wikipedia contributors, "Aether theories," *Wikipedia, The Free Encyclopedia*, https://

en.wikipedia.org/w/index.php?title=Aether
_theories&oldid=1076920265 (accessed
December 23, 2020).

Chapter 5

1. *The Way of Lao Tzu (Tao-te ching)*, trans. Wing-tsit
Chan (New York: The Bobbs-Merrill Company,
Inc., 1963), 159.

Chapter 6

1. https://www.sciencedaily.com/terms/dna.htm
(accessed April 4, 2021).

Other Titles by Chris Prentiss
Published by Power Press

Available from your favorite neighborhood and online bookstores

Zen and the Art of Happiness

The Alcoholism and Addiction Cure:
A Holistic Approach to Total Recovery
By Chris Prentiss & Pax Prentiss

Be Who You Want, Have What You Want:
Change Your Thinking, Change Your Life

The Laws of Love: Creating the Relationship
of Your Dreams

Meditation on the Perfect You
Audio

The Little Book of Secrets:
Gentle Wisdom for Joyful Living

God's Game: A God's Eye View of
You and the World
E-book. Read or listen for free here:
https://b.passagesmalibu.com/gods-game-chris-prentiss/

Goin' Home
Full-length feature film, written and directed by
Chris Prentiss. Available at GoinHomeMovie.com

I Ching Books and Gift Sets by Wu Wei:

The I Ching: The Book of Answers

**I Ching Wisdom: Guidance from
the Book of Answers, Volume I**

**I Ching Wisdom: More Guidance from
the Book of Answers, Volume II**

I Ching Readings: Interpreting the Answers

I Ching Life: Becoming Your Authentic Self

**A Tale of the I Ching: How the Book
of Changes Began**

The I Ching Workbook
The entire text of The I Ching: The Book of Answers
with 100 workbook pages to record your answers

The I Ching Gift Set
Includes Wu Wei's popular version of The I Ching:
The Book of Answers *plus 7" yarrow stalks*

The I Ching Workbook Deluxe Gift Set
Includes The I Ching Workbook *plus 10" yarrow stalks,
sandalwood incense, incense holder, silk I Ching cloth*

For bookstores:
Books and gifts sets are available at all major wholesalers
and SCB Distributors: 1-800-729-6423 or 310-532-9400

For foreign and translation rights:
Contact Yorwerth Associates
E-mail: nigel@publishingcoaches.com

Zen and the Art of Happiness
by Chris Prentiss

A timeless work about the art of happiness, the way of happiness, the inner game of happiness

Cutting-edge science and spirituality tell us that what we believe, think, and feel actually determine the makeup of our body at the cellular level. In *Zen and the Art of Happiness*, you will learn *how* to think and feel so that *what* you think and feel creates happiness and vibrancy in your life rather than gloominess or depression. You'll learn how to adapt to life's inevitable changes, how to deal with stress in a healthy way, and how to nurture a mindful happiness in your daily life.

Published in 35 foreign editions. Available in paperback, hardcover deluxe gift edition, audiobook.

CHRIS PRENTISS is the author of several popular books on personal growth, including *Zen and the Art of Happiness; Be Who You Want, Have What You Want; The Alcoholism and Addiction Cure; The Little Book of Secrets;* and *The Laws of Love*. He has also written a series of books on the wisdom of the I Ching under his pen name, Wu Wei, including his popular edition of the I Ching, entitled *The I Ching: The Book of Answers*.

Chris Prentiss is the cofounder along with his son Pax of the world-renowned Passages Addiction Cure Centers, the first non-twelve-step centers for overcoming addiction and alcoholism. He also wrote, produced, and directed the feature film *Goin' Home*. To learn more about Chris Prentiss and his work, visit chrisprentiss.com.